# How Any Woman Can Get Rich Fast in Real Estate

# How Any Woman
# Can Get Rich Fast
# in Real Estate

## Margaret Crispen

WARNER BOOKS

A Warner Communications Company

WARNER BOOKS EDITION

Copyright © 1978 by Margaret Crispen

This Warner Books Edition is published by arrangement with Andrews and McMeel, Inc.

Warner Books, Inc., 75 Rockefeller Plaza, New York, N. Y. 10019

 A Warner Communications Company

Printed in the United States of America
First Printing: March 1980
10 9 8 7 6 5 4 3 2 1

**Library of Congress Cataloging in Publication Data**

Crispen, Margaret.
    How any woman can get rich fast in real estate.

    1.   Women in real estate—United States.
I.   Title.
[HD1375.C67 1980]      333.3′3′024042      79-22677
ISBN 0-446-97254-1

# Contents

How Any Woman Can Get Rich Fast
in Real Estate

# CHAPTER 1

## The Most Fantastic Career in the World for a Woman

*Sometimes I have to pinch myself to make sure it's true. I made more than the prime minister of New Zealand last year.*

Margot Faustbiender,
Beverly Hills

From twenty to eighty, women are playing monopoly with real money. Their entrée to recognition and financial success beyond most women's wildest dreams is a slip of paper obtainable in each of our fifty states. A license to sell real estate.

There are women making $100,000 a year selling homes. Annual incomes of twenty to fifty thousand dollars are being earned in residential sales in all areas of the country.

"But, residential sales is only the tip of the iceberg," said a woman recently returned from Western Europe, where she participated in a $40 million exchange involving several thousand acres of American land and foreign commercial holdings.

Women have moved from three bedrooms and two baths to six-figure commercial complexes; to land sales

1

involving millions of dollars, and five-figure commissions. They are boarding planes to consummate international sales or exchanges; flying to Guam, Fiji, Taiwan, Saipan, Yap, or Palau to appraise resort-oriented projects, shopping centers and industrial properties for banks, loan companies, and developers—for lucrative fees. They are found in other such salaried or fee areas as property management and sales management. Ten years ago, Basalle Wong operated a tiny corner grocery store on San Francisco's Geary Boulevard; today she flies to Hong Kong and Taipei in her role of investment counselor to overseas Chinese—and has a six-figure income. A Florida woman developed a planned community and picked up a profit of over a million dollars. Not content with selling homes, some women are now building them as well. "You have three ways to go," said Helen Scott, president of the Ohio firm Helen Scott Custom Homes. "Three ways to make money. Your client usually has a home to sell. You list it. He needs a lot. You sell him the lot. Then you build his new home on the lot you've sold him. Beautiful!"

Is it *who* you know? Sometimes. Susan Goldwater listed and sold former President Ford's home, and women with celebrity connections sell the million dollar estates of rock stars and screen stars. But Lyn Dakin came to this country from England, and without any contacts sold $2.75 million worth of property on California's Palos Verdes peninsula during her first year in the business.

And, an increasing number of women are using their licenses to heed Marshall Field's advice: "Buying real estate is not only the best way, the quickest way, and the safest way, but the only way to become wealthy." Some of the largest investment percentage profits today are being made by women who started out with $1,000 to

$10,000 nest eggs, according to a Honolulu broker. "Nest eggs saved from commissions they earned in this business."

"We don't have to battle for equal pay for equal work in this business," a 22-year-old June graduate said. "There's no rule, thank God, that if a sale is made by a man the commission will be 6 percent, if by a woman, 3 percent."

Helen Hirt, a past president of the Women's Council, National Association of Realtors, and vice-president of administration for a large Midwest firm, emphasizes the point: "Real estate is one field where women always have received equal pay for equal work."

Other women point out another plus, a built-in hedge against inflation. "Based on the 6 percent commission rate, the average fee for selling a house in Montvale, New Jersey, jumped from $4,050.00 to $5,114.00 in one year," said Dorothy Martin, president of Hearthstone Gallery of Homes. In Atlanta, a house bought for $42,500 in 1969 sold for $73,000 in 1977. In Northbrook, Illinois, a house bought for $38,000 in 1964 sold for a staggering $117,000 in 1977. And in housing's "Land of Oz," a three bedroom, two bath California bungalow bought for $61,000 in 1974, turned over twice (with a 6 percent commission involved each time), and sold for $131,500 in 1977. In the Washington, D.C., suburbs, and in some areas of Southern California, home prices are rising at the rate of 2 percent per month. The median price of a home for the year 1977 rose a record 14.2 percent over the 1976 figure. This indicates an average rise of $100 per week for the single family dwelling. And more homes were sold in 1977 than in any year in the nation's history! Land values (involving a 10 percent commission) on a national average have doubled in the last five years. In thirteen states they have doubled in four years or less. Real estate professionals, according to economist Elliot Janeway, "are riding the hottest turnover market for existing property in history."

As the price of property rises, incomes rise—and without the indignity of carrying a picket sign!

With government statistics indicating the average single woman will work forty-eight years of her life, the average married woman twenty-three, women are abandoning less rewarding careers to enter real estate in unprecedented numbers. In California alone, approximately thirty-five thousand will take the examination for sales agent in the current year. Among those thirty-five thousand applicants will be teachers, nurses, lab technicians, models, ministers' wives, social workers, secretaries, twenty-two-year-old university business majors, women executives tired of commuting, thirty-year-old wives tired of making cakes for PTA bake sales—and sixty-year-old wives tired of retired husbands.

A divorcee described her frustrations in the job market before entering real estate. "I was so damn tired of lying about my age on applications. Tired of being asked about my experience—none; my education—very little; number of children and their ages. Even what my ex-husband did for a living."

When real estate was in its infancy a new commandment was added to the ten better known ones. *"All women entering real estate shalt engage solely in the sale of residential property, and shalt not covet the prerogative of man to engage in whatsoever area he damn well pleaseth."* The commandment is still in force in some offices, but most professionals agree that the custom of arbitrarily assuming that all women are best suited to selling houses is "unsound" in polite terms—"inane" in less civil language. However, the majority of women entering the business willingly observe the eleventh commandment, believing that starting out in residential sales is to their advantage. "Because that's where the big turnover is to be found—the quick action that will bring you the psychological lift of an early commission."

It is estimated that women are now responsible for 70 percent of all residential property sales throughout the nation. "I started out with an all male office," a male broker recalled. "Someone talked me into hiring a woman. I now have 120 women—and one man."

Ebby Halliday of Dallas has sold a house a day for twenty-five years A Los Angeles woman had sales totaling $1,198,000 in one month. Another Southern California woman, Helen Trimbicki, has sold $30 million worth of residential real estate in eight years. Twenty-eight years ago, a young mother of two followed her serviceman husband to Washington, D.C. Today she heads a real estate firm employing three to four thousand people, doing an annual business of $150 to $160 million. Ann Clark and Carol Delzer are both successful active residential brokers. One is in her eighties, the other in her twenties.

Signs of female success line the nation's streets, shattering myths of sex, race, age, experience and education. Call Dorothy Nakamura in Sacramento; Octavene Oberthier in Texarkana. In Honolulu, call Remy Riborozo, ex-school teacher from the Philippines. Call Antoinette Hatfield for a million-dollar embassy residence in Washington, D.C.; Mildred Sharp for a $30,000 home in Jonesboro, Arkansas; Bernice Rappaport for a million-dollar home with show business blood lines in Beverly Hills; Myrtle Hudson for a $20,000 home in Oakland, California. They sell a way of life that implies a traditional female role—and they believe in their product!

This wholehearted belief in the product, many men feel, accounts for their phenomenal success in an industry once labeled "men only."

## *Is real estate for you?*
## *Basic requirements for success.*

A woman able to pass her state's examination for real estate sales agent will find that in addition to that slip of legal paper, she must have ego-drive, empathy, enthusiasm, self-confidence, energy, initiative, the ability to work long, inconvenient hours without supervision, and a respectable supply of fortitude, replenishable under all circumstances, day or night. If she meets these considerable requirements, her broker-sponsor will probably not care whether she's twenty or sixty; Phi Beta Kappa, or dropped out of eighth grade to have the first of eight illegitimate children.

## *How to get into the business.*

Hundreds of colleges and universities now offer one or more courses in real estate. At many, students may earn a bachelor's degree with a major in real estate. A few offer advanced degrees in the field. Night-school courses are offered at high schools and junior colleges throughout the country and are usually taught by brokers from the community. While these courses are informative and interesting, they are not basically designed to prepare you for the licensee examination.

Most women come into real estate through the private real estate school geared specifically toward preparing the student for the state examination. It is estimated that 80 to 90 percent of private school students pass the exam the first time compared with an average pass rate of 50 percent.

Tuition at private schools generally runs from $135 to $200. The course can be completed in a few weeks, or may take longer, depending upon the amount of free time you have, and your study habits. At some schools each class is taught as a complete "minicourse," making it possible for students to start anytime, varying their hours and days of attendance.

Different types of moneyback guarantees such as allowing a student nine months to a year in which to repeat the course as often as is necessary to pass the exam are offered. If the student does not pass within this time period some schools, including the highly successful Anthony and Lumbleau schools, found throughout California, refund a student's tuition.

The words ownership, appraisal, taxes, finance, contracts, land, subdivision, and encumbrance will become as familiar as perhaps once were Jane, Spot, see, Dick, and run.

Under the heading "ownership" you'll find: classes of property, estates in property, ways to convey or acquire property, leases, ways to hold title, title protection.

Before you take your examination you will be able to discuss liens, easements, metes and bounds, expressed vs. implied, institutional lenders, analysis characteristics, executory vs. executed, parol or written, eminent domain, and a host of other subjects and terms related to the industry.

Length and complexity of the examination will vary in individual states, though in recent years an effort has been made to make the examination as uniform as differing state laws allow. As an example, California's applicants are given three and one-half hours to answer one hundred and fifty questions.

Women in the business warn that on-going education is required because of industry changes and complexities. Organized real estate on the national, state, and local level sees to it that there are current books, tapes, and seminars available on specific areas such as servicing listings, arranging financing, figuring closing costs, handling an offer, and opening an escrow. Information on trust-fund requirements, securities and syndication, federal taxes, and a variety of related industry subjects is at hand.

After passing your state examination you will be licensed to sell real estate under the auspices of a real estate broker, as an independent contractor. The term "independent contractor" means that the broker pays nothing toward your social security taxes, workmen's compensation, or unemployment compensation.

A typical real estate office consists of a broker—a sales manager in the larger multifirms—several sales agents, and clerical help. The firm may sell properties (residential, commercial-industrial, investment), businesses, and land; develop new building projects; arrange for loans to finance purchases; and rent properties. It is the agents who do most of the showing and selling of property.

Your income will depend entirely on commissions from your sales and from any listings you bring to the agency. Women in the business suggest that you have money to carry you for six months, usually adequate until your first commission comes through. They point out that there is usually a lapse of several weeks between sale and close of escrow.

A house that sells for $60,000 will, in most states, produce a commission of 6 percent, or $3,600. Unimproved land brings a 10 percent commission.

Customarily, the firm listing a property is entitled to

50 percent of the fee when the property is sold, the firm responsible for the sale, the other half. Of the listing broker's share, one-half goes to the listing agent. The agent responsible for the sale is entitled to one-half of her firm's share.

The fifty-fifty split is usually the best arrangement a beginning agent can work out with a broker, but as your volume of business increases, you will be in a position to ask for and receive a higher percentage of the fee on a house you list or sell. Top producers sometimes progress to a ninety-ten commission split with their broker.

Had you, a new agent, sold the $60,000 home, your part of the commission would have been roughly $900. Had you listed the home for your firm, and sold it, your share would have been roughly $1,800. Had you been both broker, lister, and seller, the entire $3,600 would have been yours.

Your firm will provide you, its sales agent, with desk, telephone, and clerical help; keep you up-to-date on changes in listings and finance; and pick up the tab for the ads you write to advertise a home you have listed, or one which you wish to try to sell. As a new, inexperienced agent, you will find your advertising somewhat restricted.

You, in turn, will be expected to maintain an up-to-date, full-size, air-conditioned sedan to transport your customers from neighborhood to neighborhood, house to house. Some agencies provide their salespeople with a back-up car for emergencies, pick up the tab for license fees, business cards, and personalized HOUSE FOR SALE signs. But, such largesse is not typical.

### An essential step.

Patty Mattoon entered real estate in 1958 in

Pittsburgh, Pennsylvania, received her broker's license in the early 1960s, and formed her own company. While serving as the Greater Pittsburgh Board of Realtors' first woman president in its 64 year history, Patty's primary objective was "making incoming professionals aware of the importance of membership in the 575,000-member National Association of Realtors, and making the public aware of the value of the Realtor (broker) designation and Realtor Associate (agent) designation." Realtor, she explained, is a registered trademark and is always capitalized.

"What are the advantages of membership?" I asked.

"There is the very obvious advantage of the education programs offered by the association, and its various institutes—Farm and Land, Real Estate Management, Securities and Syndication, etc.

"And, most boards now sponsor hospitalization, life insurance, blood bank, and home inspection programs —all of benefit to the licensee."

Consumerism, said Patty Mattoon, is placing greater demands on the real estate industry today, and this is another reason she feels it imperative that all brokers and salespersons be members of their local boards.

"The National Association adopted a Code of Ethics in 1913 which demands that we take care of people fairly and honestly. The code hasn't changed drastically over the years because it has always placed the emphasis on the importance of treating clients in this manner."

### What you can expect to make— starting out in residential sales.

You will be limited only by your ability to deal successfully with your clients, by the amount of time you devote to the business; to some extent by the price of properties you choose to sell.

Lucy Bell, selling in the Hancock Park area of Los Angeles, where homes range in price from $100,000 to $500,000, has had an annual income of $100,000 for several years. Joan Thomas of the Nancy Reynolds Agency of Westfield, New Jersey, sells less expensive homes, but a larger number, and for her efforts has an annual income of between $30,000 and $40,000. Loretta Sokol of Anchorage, Alaska, who moved from saleswoman to sales manager, with twelve men and twelve women under her tutelage, feels that a woman entering the field in Anchorage should earn $20,000 a year—upward of that as she builds a clientele. "She should give herself a year. If she can't reach that figure and go above it, she's probably in the wrong business in Anchorage."

Virgie Turner is a black woman Realtor doing business in a Los Angeles district where the homes range from $18,000 to $35,000.

"What could a new saleswoman expect to make if she went to work for you?" I asked.

"If she worked full-time, I'd expect her to average at least $1,200 a month in her first year. That's based on selling $20,000 properties. The commission on a $20,000 home is $1,200. Two sales a month would give her around $1,200."

"Suppose she hadn't listed either of those two houses. She'd only get $300 a house, or a total of $600."

"Sometimes you'll sell another agent's listing, while they're selling yours. It'll average out—if you're out there working."

"By 'out there working,' do you mean coming into the office every day?"

"Honey, no woman is going to make any money sitting in this little office on Manchester Boulevard—or in some fancy place on Wilshire Boulevard. 'Out there working' means getting out with the people—handing out your card, talking to people, listening, looking at houses.

"When you're coming in new, you ought to go to a different beauty shop every week for your hair, so you can leave your card. Shop at different markets, and leave your card with the checkers. Hand out your card with everything you buy—your gas, your clothes. Let your friends know you're in the business. Ask them to list with you. A woman can live on her listings."

Much will depend on your location. Lizabeth Wade sells homes in Florence, Alabama, a small city in the northern area of the state. "We don't make as much here as the women do in Birmingham and Montgomery. There isn't the demand, and the prices are not as high. But then we don't spend as much." Artha Garza sells properties in Dallas, Texas, ranging from $100,000 to one million dollars. (Two of her sales were for cash— one for $185,000 and one for $240,000.) But, contrary to rumor, Dallas's streets are not teeming with booted, spurred buyers prodding women to find them $100,000 homes, whereas agents in house-starved Fairbanks, Alaska, sometimes list a property in the morning and sell it before noon.

*Question: Where can you go from residential sales?*
*Answer: Anywhere.*

Like hundreds of other women you can become a broker. In some states, by law, you must have at least two years' experience selling, plus a growing amount of formal education in order to be eligible for the broker's examination. In others, you may take the examination any time you feel you can pass it.

While some women prefer to remain in the role of agent (incomes of $20,000 to $100,000 quoted were earned by agents working through brokers as independent contractors), the number of women brokers is increasing steadily throughout the country. Some prefer to remain small, operating a one-person office with an answering service, or with one to six agents working with them. Other women have elected to expand to the multifirm class with sales managers operating branch offices.

Your ratio of dollar income to number of transactions will be huge by comparison with a retail business. And, you will not be ordering merchandise from a manufacturer, stocking shelves, and wondering whether your selection will sell. Your merchandise costs you nothing. The shelves your merchandise sits on are the streets, boulevards, drives, and country roads across the nation. And, your sales force works on commission. You'll have such expenses as listing and advertising fees, clerical salaries, utilities, and rent, but you will be free of the two heaviest expenses incurred by the retail businessman—inventory and labor.

Once you have your broker's license, you may want to specialize. Through the National Association of Realtors' education program, many fields are open to you. Like Mary Lou Melville, of Montana, you can earn the right to use the initials, AFLB (Accredited Farm and Land Broker). Mary Lou is also a member of the Society of Exchange Counselors, and exchanges properties world-wide, Europe, Tahiti, Canada, Mexico, the Orient. Most of Mary Lou's transactions are for a million dollars or more.

Or perhaps you feel like Charis Zeigler of the Zeigler

Company of California: "I could not get excited about sunny kitchens, where to put someone else's piano or grandmother, or how far fat Freddie had to walk to school." If you find that her words could have been taken from your mouth, you can follow her, and a growing number of career-conscious women, into commercial-industrial investment real estate.

You can join a select group pioneering a new field for women—real estate appraising. "Most women think they can't measure out a house," said VA Appraiser Kay Murray of Los Angeles. "But, we've been cutting out patterns for years, and it's a lot harder to make a dress than measure a house. Appraising is a natural for women."

Like Gladys Chretien, a black broker of Los Angeles, you can become an entrepreneur. Gladys is owner of her own real estate company, part-owner of Washington Escrow Company, Washington Reconveyance Corporation, Wall Street Enterprises, and Manchester Mortgage Company.

If a base salary appeals to you, become a sales manager like Marian Pozdol of Illinois and Phyllis Hillebrand of Connecticut. Or, become one of a handful of women designated CPM (Certified Property Manager).

You can follow Mary Harpley of Ohio into residential contracting, Dixie Williams of Florida into developing. If you identify with people who prefer houses built in 1860, reconverted streetcar barns, and carriage houses, you can form a company similar to Restorations, Incorporated, of San Antonio and specialize in historic restorations.

If you're uninterested in closets and cupboards, consider office leasing, along with Marilyn Wolfe of Atlanta, Jan Campbell of Honolulu, and a growing number of younger women.

Where can you go? Mary Shern went to Honolulu and opened her own real estate school. Carol Griffin went to the Virgin Islands, and flies her clients from St. Thomas to St. Croix to St. John. Maxine DeBoer went to Alaska, and Billie Ross came home to California.

If the idea that the real estate industry is controlled organizationally by men bothers you—put your pumps or sandals in the leadership door alongside Anna Graff's of Alaska, Patty Mattoon's of Pittsburgh, Barbara Carver's of Houston.

## Why women fail.

With some women "rollerskating" up and down the nation's streets, across farms and developments, through industrial complexes, supermarkets, warehouses, hotel lobbies and barns—why do other women fail so miserably and drop out?

No one stands at the door marked "EXIT" with counter in hand, but industry lore estimates that half of the women entering real estate drop out in the first year, and that 90 percent are out in five years. A high failure rate, women point out, is inevitable in a business with such ease of entry.

William North, general counsel for the National Association of Realtors, describes real estate as a "free enterprise business which rewards success but does not countenance failure." He warns that the relationship between independent contractor and broker is one which measures productivity in absolute terms. "No credit is given for hours spent; no merit seen in unsuccessful effort; no virtue recognized in future activity."

According to a study made by Herbert and Jeanne Greenberg of Marketing Survey and Research, Princeton, New Jersey, two qualities are "absolutely necessary" for success in real estate sales. Ego-drive and empathy. The first, ego-drive, the Greenbergs stress, is not necessarily ambition, aggression, or even willingness to work—but the desire and need to *persuade*, not for money, or other rewards, but for the satisfaction that comes from victory.

The top women producers in some offices, I learned, do not need money. "Don't misunderstand me," a Texas woman in residential sales said. "I like to make money. But—and you'll probably classify me as a liar—that's not the most important part. Recognition. That's the thing that turns so many women on in this business, the reason so many are successful."

Empathy, the second quality the Greenbergs found to be an absolute necessity, is the rare capacity to recognize clues and cues thrown out by people. The woman in real estate who has the ability to get feedback from her clients is able to adjust her behavior and sales talk— even her mode of dress.

Of all the reasons for failure, the one most often expressed by women and men alike was "the belief of some women that they can 'dabble' in real estate part-time."

A successful Pennsylvania woman reveals that she spends at least fifty hours a week on the job. And Lucy Bell, of Los Angeles, speaking of friends who have confided that they, too, might like to dabble in real estate, said: "I don't think they have any idea how hard I work." She recalled the night she was up until three A.M. driving Los Angeles freeways between buyer and seller, delivering and redelivering counter offers.

Searching for a contact willing to speak frankly if promised immunity from her fellow professionals, her local board, her clients, and the IRS, I found "Mona."

She was thirty-five years old, she said, divorced with

two children. She entered real estate as a residential agent eight years ago. After two years in residential sales, she changed firms to one specializing in commercial-industrial properties, studied for a broker's license, and opened her own commercial-industrial firm.

"What do you think of women working part-time?" I asked.

"Hell. We had one of those in my first residential office. She'd drop in the office a couple of days a week, do her nails, talk to her friends on our business phone about her 'career' in real estate, maybe look through some travel folders. At three, she'd leave to drive her daughter to dancing school. Her name was Eloise. She works at Woolworth's now.

"Her excuse was 'being a good mother.' But, I know two top producers who are also 'good mothers.' One has nine children, one five. If a woman can't organize her kids, she has two choices—get out of real estate or put the kids in an orphanage."

"What of the woman with no nest egg who must keep her salaried job, but wants to try selling on Saturdays and Sundays?"

"Some firms won't hire her, feeling it's unfair to their regular sales force to allow 'weekenders' to skim the cream off. But if she perseveres she may find a good firm willing to give her a chance. And some of these women really go to town, and are secure enough to give up their eight-to-five jobs in a short time."

"What are some of the other reasons women fail?"

"They fail for all sorts of reasons because, God, you wouldn't believe some of the women we get in this business! In the early seventies, during the 'miniskirt' years, we had a girl named Anita in the office for three weeks. Her hair was longer than her skirt, and her false eyelashes longer than her nose. I'm sure there was an 'Anita' in every office in town—for three weeks.

"And, we get our share of femme fatales—women who insist on answering the phone with fake, throaty voices. When they're not watching the door for a man, they study the latest sex manual—while the rest of the women study the latest tax change.

"Then we have the unprincipled, avaricious—the 'Jaws in Skirts.' They don't last any longer than the Anitas and the Eloises. You've got to have the respect of the people you work with, as well as your client's. This business is built on referrals.

"Some women fail simply because they're women," she said seriously. "They haven't the confidence it takes to succeed in the business world. They can't delegate authority, make decisions, lead.

"So many women have hang-ups. If a woman thinks she's handicapped because she's a woman—she's handicapped! She'll fail for sure."

"What about age? When is a woman too old to consider real estate?"

"When she's in a wheelchair and diagnosed as an advanced case of senility.

"But, if she *thinks* she's too old at fifty or sixty, she's too old. No doubt about it. I know a great woman in this business who is eighty-two. Tell her she's too old, and she'll tell you that anyone under sixty is too young to handle money. She came in at sixty, incidentally."

"What's too young?"

"The same thing applies to the young girls coming in out of college, junior college, or high school. You can get a license at eighteen, you know, although I'm not sure I approve. Some of the very young do remarkably well. But, if they think no one will buy a house from them because they're too young, they're damn right. No one will. But, there are twenty-two-year-old girls who have their broker's license, and have people selling for them."

"What about education? Is lack of education a handicap?"

"If a woman thinks she has a problem because she doesn't have a college education—she has a real problem. But, some of the sharpest women in this business didn't have a chance to graduate from high school. They don't know they have a problem.

"And, if a woman thinks she's handicapped because she isn't beautiful—she's the ugliest woman in the world. There's a woman in this business who sells an unbelievable amount of property—something like four million dollars a year. Meet her in the hall and you'd think she was the cleaning woman. Heavy features, thin hair, and, God, she must weigh two hundred pounds! But, if it bothers her you'd never know it. She's right in there with Miss America."

"Any other reasons for failure?"

"Sometimes a successful woman fails intentionally. My top producer went for months without a sale, and didn't seem to care. I got to the bottom of it and found she had problems at home. She had been making a great deal more money than her husband, and it was wrecking her marriage. She was deliberately failing because she didn't want her husband to feel emasculated."

"Now that we've covered failure, do you have a prescription for success?"

"To succeed in real estate a woman has to remember that she's a businesswoman. That covers her relations with her husband, children, and clients; her dress, behavior, and outlook.

"She's not a doormat for a man, or a sexy siren, or president of the PTA. If she wants to play office she can buy a desk, have the telephone company run a spur in, put her typewriter on the desk, and get an 'in' box and an 'out' box. But that's not real estate."

## Three questions.

Have you married the right man, one who will not feel emasculated if you happen to make more money than he does? Have you taken care to bear children who will not put the cat in the dryer while you're trying to close a sale that will pay you $10,000? And, most important, are you that rare woman in today's security-conscious world willing to give up the solid feel of a salary under your feet for the chance to soar as far, as high, as your own ego-driven, empathizing wings will take you? The most fantastic career in the world for a woman can be yours!

# CHAPTER 2

## A Look at the Past.
## What Was It Like?
## "Like Hell!"

HOUSEHOLD HELP WTD.

*Fine upstanding gentleman seeks
fine upstanding woman for purposes
of marriage and bearing children.
Must have reliable physical qualities
incl. strong back, arms, legs. Duties to
include caring for lrg. 5 bdr. house,
grnds., and stbl. Must have sense hmr.
and play musc. instrum. Two wks.
vacation at mountains every June. Gd.
future. Apl. on or before Aug. 23,
1908, to Box 235, San Fran., Calif. No
woman who talks loudly in
restaurants, reads romantic novels or
smokes cigarettes need apply.*

"Go home, lady, and mend your husband's socks,"
was the reported rebuff a woman received upon attempting to enter a Washington, D.C., law school
shortly after the Civil War.

No National Organization for Women, no Women's Caucus, no Consumer Affairs for Women (very few affairs of the more traditional type—none in some cases). Getting a foot in real estate's door without suffering mangled toes was no more difficult than getting a feminine foot in the door of any other area—except the kitchen.

In 1892, a Texas woman, Cora Foster, had the temerity to open a real estate office in Houston; and the further temerity to found the first Houston real estate board. In that same year, she helped found the first national body in the real estate field, the short-lived National Real Estate Association, a predecessor of the present-day National Association of Realtors.

Here, real estate's record of "Miss Cora's" exploits ends—as abruptly as her aborted National Real Estate Association. When the National Association of Real Estate Boards was formed sixteen years later, in 1908, the stenographic record shows no mention of Miss Cora—or any other woman. Local real estate boards, composed solely of men, were the sole judge of qualifications for membership. In some younger and smaller boards, a few qualified women were included. They came largely from three groups: a relatively few outstanding individual pioneers (widows or daughters carrying on male-established businesses); mother-son or husband-wife combinations; and women who began as rental agents or office workers and who in time of emergency—or because of their own dogged determination—were pressed into service as agents or brokers.

Who was the first woman to be admitted to membership in the National Association? A search of old membership files reveals the names of two women admitted in 1912—Corinne Simpson of Seattle and Frances Wines of St. Louis. Another source shows the first recorded application of a woman for membership in a real estate board was made by an Omaha, Nebraska, woman in 1911. It was accepted, but her name was not entered in the national roster. A second application for membership was made by a Detroit woman that same year. Turned down.

The Women's Council of Realtors was organized in 1939, ironically enough, because a man became interested in what women were doing. Joseph Catherine of Brooklyn, president of the National Association in 1938, was impressed by the work being done by the state women's division in California, and saw the need for more qualified women in the profession.

"In England," Mr. Catherine said, "women engaged in the real estate field have a separate organization because none of the three real estate associations in that country admit women to membership." He expressed the opinion that such a separate organization was not needed in this country, "since most of the real estate boards, though there are exceptions, now permit women to hold active membership." Actually, the council was to find that this meant most boards had no rule *against* women, but "just weren't ready for it."

The Women's Council was not, at its founding, and is not, presently, a separate organization—but a part of the National Association of Realtors.

Women, say council leaders, often enter real estate with little or no previous business background. The council, at the local, state, and national level, they contend, provides the opportunity for members to share experiences and to discuss problems and, through this dialogue, secure support from one another.

A majority of today's active women do not hold mem bership in the council, feeling that it tends to set women aside as a group; however, few will argue that it served as an essential instrument in elevating the standards of women in the business, encouraging the selection of qualified women, and gaining recognition for the accomplishments of women.

Hanna Freud, of New York City, who died in December 1926 at age seventy-six, probably did more to gain recognition and acceptance for women in the field of real estate than any other woman. Entering the business before the turn of the century, Miss Freud specialized in renting. Of necessity. (It was considered unladylike, possibly defeminizing, for a woman to engage in sales. She could, however, engage in renting or leasing property without risking growing a beard or having her voice drop several octaves.)

New York's Twenty-third Street shopping center, established around 1910, gave Hanna her big opportunity—a way to break out of residential rentals and into commercial leasing. Several years later, guessing that the city would move northward, she convinced her merchant clients of the sagacity of her intuition and was able to relocate a number of them—assuring her own financial security with the proceeds from the lucrative leases. It is said that Miss Freud closed more leases for the Shattuck Company, owner of the Schrafft stores, than any other broker. A fall on the ice at sixty-six left her crippled, but she remained active until her death, ten years later—using cabs to cross and recross the city and its burroughs. She maintained both home and office in New York's Hotel Commodore, from the day the hotel opened until her death.

A search of her files revealed that she was in the midst of negotiations for the lease and sale of several properties when she died.

New York in the early twenties provided the backdrop for success for several female real estate pioneers. Josephine Schaefer entered the business as a stenographer during that period, and rose to the position of vice-president and director of one of the ten largest brokerage firms in New York. Lillian Moebus, upon her graduation from Columbia University, also entered the industry as a stenographer during the twenties. Years later, when she was president of a large Brooklyn firm, she recalled that her first employer had advised her, "In the future, choose a women's college—not Columbia— from which to graduate." Lena Goldstein, also of Brooklyn, entered real estate in 1925 and became the second woman to qualify for membership in the American Institute of Appraisers. (The first was a California woman— L. Crawford.)

Since most women engaged in real estate today are also investing in their product, no history of women in the industry would be complete without a word about real estate investor Hetty Green of New York City. Hetty was conceded to be the shrewdest, coolest, most calculating investor of her time—also the rudest, stingiest, and sloppiest.

In the wintertime, Hetty's contemporaries—with only one or two million dollars between them and the Bowery—recklessly hailed five-dollar cabs for transportation to glittering affairs, while Hetty pulled a pair of coarse stockings over her stout shoes and tramped through the snow to her destination, pulling off the stockings when she arrived and spreading them on the startled hostess's hatrack to dry. When she did not walk, she traveled on streetcars around the city. But, not on her own money—on transfers she picked up from the streets. Business associates recalled that her old worn handbag was so stuffed with crumpled, foraged transfers it was almost impossible for her to find anything in the bag. When her daughter married the grandson of John Jacob Astor in 1909, Hetty made her own brief social splurge—exchanged her cheap flat in Hoboken where she had lived for many years for an expensive suite at the Plaza.

## WANTED: Boy to handle rentals.

In 1925, young Vera Rivers answered an ad in a Berkeley, California, paper for: "Boy to handle rentals on commission basis" and talked the owner of the brokerage firm into hiring her—without requiring her to submit to a sex change. "You're not allowed to sell," her broker employer warned. "That's for men only."

"I had to have a license from the California State Real Estate Department," she said. "The license said I was a salesman, but the broker didn't see it that way. At any rate," she added philosophically, "he *did* pay for the license."

"How much?"

"Two dollars."

Average Berkeley rentals ran around $50.00 a month in 1925, Vera said. "The company got 25 percent of the first month's rent, and I got one-half of that amount; a $6.25 commission for a $50.00 rental."

She opened a ledger and thumbed through it. "That first month, I made $79.69, but here's a month I made $283.76. That was big money for a young girl in 1925. My average for the year was $184.52 a month."

"Of course, that didn't all come from the rentals. The O.K. Moving Company of Berkeley gave me a percentage of their fee if I recommended them to my renters and they got the job. And, if I sent renters who also had to have furniture to the Jackson Furniture Company, they gave me a percentage of the total purchase."

She turned the ledger to another page. "The company also reimbursed me for my gas and oil. In October 1925, I bought $7.76 cents worth of gas and oil. Five gallons of gas cost ninety cents, and five gallons of gas and two quarts of oil cost $1.40."

On Labor Day, 1927, all males in the firm took a well-deserved holiday, and Vera was left to hold the office open—with instructions that if anyone was interested in buying: "Take their name and number, honey, so that one of the men can contact them Tuesday morning."

"Two couples came in together looking for rentals. I took them out and showed them everything we had, but they weren't satisfied with any of the places. On the way back to the office, we passed a subdivision the company was handling. The homes sold for $6,000, with $500 down, and payments of $50 a month. My renters liked the look of the homes from the outside.

"I explained that they were not for rent, but they insisted on seeing them.

"When we came out, both couples wanted to buy one. I stopped in one of the company's branch offices, asked the girl holding it open for a sales agreement—told her they just wanted to look at it—went around the corner, and wrote the two sales up on the hood of my 1925 Ford roadster. They each gave me $500 for a down payment.

"Well, I really got the devil for that the next day. My broker said the men in the office needed the money more than I did. I couldn't quite figure out why, because I wasn't married, any more than some of the men, and I was supporting my mother. My broker gave me 5 percent commission on the two $500 deposits (the male salesmen got 3 percent of the total $6,000 price) and warned me, 'Don't ever do that again!' "

In 1929, when the Depression hit, rentals dropped to $25 a month in Berkeley—and still stood vacant. "I couldn't make enough to live on," Vera said.

She worked for a salary for several years, but was never able to make more than $160 a month—less than she had been averaging as a rental "boy." The months in Berkeley had convinced her that a woman's best chance for income lay in real estate. "I was determined to get back into it as soon as I could."

## Kitchen and curbstone brokerage

Although men brokers seldom hired women as agents, California law was more understanding— permitting a woman to obtain a broker's license if she could pass the examination and pay the fee. Vera studied for her broker's license while working at other jobs and in 1940 passed the state examination, paid a five-dollar fee, and became a licensed broker.

"There were a number of women brokers in the San Francisco area during those years, operating from their homes. We'd go out and ring doorbells, asking owners if they'd like to sell their homes. We'd place little ads in the paper, and phone one another about our listings. I lived at 2210 Jackson Street in a one-room apartment for $75 a month. Sometimes, I'd have to take the deposit money in the hall, because I didn't want to invite a man into my bedroom. They called us 'Kitchen Brokers' or 'Curbstoners.'

"There were women kitchen or curbstone brokers throughout the country in those days. Organized real estate wasn't very happy with us, and that is easily understood. But for some of us, it was the only way we could get in."

In 1945, she crossed the Golden Gate Bridge to Marin County and rented a tiny frame building on Redhill Road in San Anselmo for $50 a month, sharing the rent with three other women brokers. "The men called it the

'Hen's Nest.' We had ruffled curtains at the front window. From the street, it probably looked more like someone's kitchen than a business office."

Vera became one of growing Marin County's most successful and respected Realtors—not only selling and listing properties, but building subdivisions. She lost her hearing in 1960 and was forced into semiretirement.

"I have a partner now who runs the firm, but I can still take listings from old clients and friends and write the ads," she said. "I don't show property any more, because I can't get around too well.

"That's the great thing about this business. Working, keeping active, keeps a woman young. And, in this business, you decide when you want to retire. No one else."

## *"I thought we'd gone to hell when we elected you."*

The words are octogenarian Helen Nixon's, quoting an unspecified male upon her election as a director of the Evanston, Illinois, Board of Realtors in 1951.

Helen graduated from Northwestern, Class of 1919, and entered real estate as a secretary in 1924.

"It's no wonder the men were wary. Requirements were so lax for licensing as to be almost nonexistent. Some women came in so uninformed they gave the business a bad name. But I was encouraged by men to get my broker's license. They thought my secretarial background with a leading brokerage firm gave me an excellent working knowledge of the business."

She pointed out that when she obtained her Illinois broker's license in 1932, there were no requirements to attend a real estate school—public or private—if such a thing existed, or to pass a written examination.

"I looked up some of the rules and bylaws before I

went before the examining board. They asked me where I lived and a question or two about joint tenancy. One of the men on the board knew the broker I'd worked for. I paid the State five or ten dollars, I can't remember exactly, and was issued a real estate broker's license for the State of Illinois.

"When we went to real estate board meetings, the women sat on one side of the room and the men on the other. If they sat down on the east side, we took the west side. But that wasn't because of discrimination. There were so few of us I think we instinctively wanted to stick together for moral support."

Today's real estate business, Helen concedes, bears little resemblance to the real estate business of 1932.

"In those days you had a prospect, you found a property he liked and could afford. Sometimes he paid cash, and sometimes you sold the property under contract— so much down and so much a month. We didn't have FHA or VA or all these percentage loans. We weren't concerned with relating so many complex things to a piece of property—tax considerations, future circumstances, labor costs, etc.

"All these rules, regulations, ordinances make becoming an agent—particularly a broker—a very difficult project now.

"Downright painful," she emphasized.

Helen lives on Gaffield Road in Evanston in a home built by her parents sixty years ago. At eighty, she remains alert and active, with no plans for retirement. "Working keeps a woman young," she said. "When I go to bed at night, I know I have something to get up for the next morning—the details of a contract to work out, a couple coming in at eleven."

Attesting to their trust and respect, in 1951 the Illinois Association of Realtors elected her its first woman director since its formation in 1908. She has also served as a director on the national level, and for several years was the only woman on the National Association's Washington committee, the legislative arm of organized real estate.

"One broker I worked for had just finished serving a jail sentence for embezzlement," said salty eighty-year-old Margaret Herbert of Los Angeles.

Entrance requirements were no stiffer for men than for women, and it seems possible that early examining boards may have gone out to lunch more frequently when assessing the lack of qualifications of a male than a female.

Another broker she worked for, said the blunt Miss Herbert, was so stingy that he had only one working telephone for ten salespeople. "The others were padlocked to save money. We had to stand in line—all ten of us to use the phone. I made $300 that year, which I thought was pretty good considering the handicaps he put in our path."

In the mid-forties, she went to Coldwell Banker, one of the town's leading firms, and talked to a "Mr. Hastings" about placing her license with the firm. Mr. Hastings, she said, made it clear that he didn't want a woman working for him, especially one who was satisfied with $300 a year. "I told him that if I'd been satisfied, I wouldn't be looking for work.

"I called him every day for three weeks and finally went back to the office to demand that he hire me or tell me to leave him alone. He must have figured that anyone as persistent as I was would make a good salesman [sic], because he hired me."

Smartly dressed and coiffed, at eighty-two Margaret Herbert has now sold homes to the wealthy and the trying-to-be wealthy for forty years in Beverly Hills, Bel Air, Holmby Hills, Brentwood, and Westwood.

"I've never been on a freeway," she confided. "They're a little fast for me at eighty-two."

Sitting in the living room of her Spanish-style home on a quiet street not far from CBS Television City, I asked her when she planned to retire.

"Never," she said emphatically. "The business is too exciting. I remember the time you wouldn't list a house if the price was out of line. Now if the sellers tell you they want $2 million and you sold that exact house in 1935 for $75,000, and two years ago for $1 million, you don't bat an eyelash, you just list it. If you don't someone else will."

## *EMANCIPATION!! Of a sort.*

The manpower shortage of World War II released women from the shackles of "rent only," and by the early fifties they were driving family sedans into real estate in sufficient numbers to cause a traffic jam. They were limited to selling homes for the most part, but it was a giant step up the "equality of opportunity ladder."

Much has been written about the young woman of the fifties (the most common observations are that she married too young and had very little premarital sexual experience). In 1951 (as in 1865, when the young lady applied for admittance to law school and was advised to go home and mend her husband's socks), there were no organizations devoted to securing a woman's right to enter the profession of her choice, earn equal pay for equal work, or burn her wired bra. In lay language, no one gave a damn. Ask the average young woman on the street in 1951 what she thought of the women's movement—after a startled moment at your brashness—she would probably have replied that she felt movement between the fourth and fifth months of her pregnancy.

Mankind, according to female real estate veterans, cared even less about securing equal rights for the middle-aged empty-nester of the fifties. If you were a middle-aged empty-nester, veterans say, it was assumed that you had served your purpose by serving your husband and children for twenty or thirty years. It was also assumed that you would bury your husband (at the appropriate time and with an appropriate amount of tears), observe lonely birthdays for another ten years in an empty nest, smile gratefully at your thoughtful children when they moved you to a retirement home, nursing home, or hospital. And die with as little fuss as possible.

If a middle-aged empty-nester—married, bored, or just plain starving to death on her widow's portion of a Social Security check—rebelled at following the established pattern, any number of glamorous opportunities awaited her because of her "background." She had been serving food for years so waiting tables was wide open—until her arches collapsed. She had spent untold hours, needle in hand, letting down or taking up hems, and patching blue jeans. Alteration rooms at the rear of "Ladies Better Dresses" could use her—until the cataracts formed. Baby-sitting was also open, but fifty cents an hour wasn't worth much in the recognition market or the supermarket—and it meant taking the hot fudge sundae out of some teenager's mouth. Some women felt well qualified as long or short distance movers, thanks to many years of on-the-job training by the time their children gave up braces and took up sex, and their husbands gave up sex and took up golf. But, the female physical makeup made the carrying and loading of furniture into vans a rather far-fetched career possibility—even for the desperate empty-nesters of the fifties. Other women felt that a career in chauffeuring might be the answer since they knew the streets, alleys, freeways, and backroads so intimately, having sped up and down their backs from baseball diamond to orthodontist; fifty miles up the canyon to Camp Willow Wee Wee to deliver forgotten female canteen; south to North High to deliver forgotten male glasses to offspring taking SAT test; home to check on eight-year-old mumps victim—and turn the heat on the roast. Unfortunately, opportunities for uniformed chauffeurs were limited in Muleshoe, Potato Slough, and Wounded Knee, and since a husband usually refused to move to West Palm or Newport to satisfy his wife's craving for financial security and recognition in uniformed chauffeuring—she found the car door slammed in her face too.

What was left? Houses were left. She had cleaned them. Nailed them. Scraped them. Painted them. She had filled their cupboards, washed their windows, scrubbed their floors, and measured their closets. She had loved them. She had cursed them. She had done everything else with them—Gad! why not sell them!?

The fifties are referred to by some women who entered the business during those years as the era when the "house woman" went out for coffee, kept the men's desks free of dust, the front windows free of fly specks, and obeyed orders to: "Run this to the bank, honey, while I take care of this client."

Del Stewart, now a condominium specialist in Northern California, went to work in a real estate office on Throckmorton Avenue in Mill Valley in 1952.

"The office didn't hire a secretary. I typed the contracts, answered the phone, made the coffee, kept the ashtrays emptied, etc. The broker-owner did not even arrange for one of the men to relieve me on the phone so I could have a lunch hour. I brought it in a bag, and ate it with one hand on the phone, while the men went out. I worked like a dog—all for free—for weeks without being given the chance to make a sale. Every time a prospect came in the door, the men jumped up and met them before I could get out from behind my typewriter."

The number of women in real estate employed as agents or brokers more than doubled during the fifties—from twenty-odd thousand in 1950 to over forty-six thousand in 1960. In 1967, it was estimated that about seventy-five thousand women were selling real estate. By 1976, over two-hundred thousand women were in some aspect of the real estate business.

*"A black woman in a white man's world*
*has to work four times as hard*
*and be twice as good."*

Some women in real estate faced a far greater challenge. "You prove to whites first that a black can do a job," said Flaxie Pinkett, president of a Washington, D.C., firm, "then you prove the same thing to your fellow blacks."

No industry, in any other nation, has given black women the opportunity for success as has American real estate. And, no group of women, in any country, at any time has grabbed the golden ring with such spectacular results. Working under the double handicap of sex and race, they have gained recognition, respect, financial security, and the opportunity to assist others up the ladder—from the early pioneers who sold two-, three-, and four-thousand-dollar homes in ghetto areas for tiny commissions to modern-day businesswomen who head brokerage firms, property management firms, mortgage and escrow firms.

Flaxie Pinkett has a concise business philosophy which she says is an absolute essential for success for the black woman. It is: "To excel."

"Handicapped by prejudice, lacking resources, and credit, you are going to compete in the open market with long-established, well-financed firms who have an abundance of everything you do not have, and who have no knowledge of the receiving end of prejudice.

"But, there are certain advantages to being in this particular predicament," she pointed out. "If you work four times as hard in order to be four times as good, the result is quite often what you might expect: a superior product that people buy, not because it's offered by a woman or a black woman, but because it's offered by a person who does a better job.

"Many times, I repeat: 'We are not a Negro business. We are a business firm owned by Negroes.'"

The John R. Pinkett firm was started in a basement office with one desk and one employee—"and no customers"—in the depths of the Depression, 1932. That same year, Flaxie Pinkett entered college at fourteen and during the next four years worked in the basement office keeping records and answering the phone after class hours and on weekends. When she graduated in 1936, at eighteen, she went to work full time in the business. In 1976, she was named Realtor of the Year by the Washington, D.C., Board of the National Association of Realtors, the first woman to be so honored and the first black.

"We found that the expertise developed in moderate-income housing is equally applicable to management of luxury apartments. We have established a reputation for the rehabilitation of urban properties, as we have in the sale of prime residential and commercial properties. We have moved from the narrow spectrum of moderate income housing to a broad spectrum of commercial and luxury units. Every customer who walks in our door gets the best service we can offer. If he is a person of moderate means who has saved some money and wants to buy a 'piece of property' for investment purposes, he receives as much care and attention as we give to a transaction involving a high-rise office building."

The firm proved itself first, in properties that are the most difficult to manage profitably for landlords—moderate-income housing where the spread between costs and revenues is slight, where maintenance costs tend to be high because of large families, and where the tenants themselves tend to be upwardly mobile but under constant financial pressure.

Flaxie Pinkett feels that the most important thing she has proven is her own competence. "When you're black—and when you're a woman, too—you can understand how important this is."

Beatrice Reed, of Silver Springs, Maryland, is another Washington area woman whose career in real estate is a miracle of modern-day business and a tribute to her ability and tenacity.

A native of the West Indies, she is an articulate, vivacious woman with a soft, musical voice. She attended Howard University until family responsibilities forced her to seek a job, and after trying teaching, insurance selling, government clerical work, and several other avenues, she ended up in real estate twenty-five years ago.

Starting out as a saleswoman, she "learned all the things I wouldn't do in the real estate business." Within eight months she was a broker, establishing a business of her own and setting up offices on Florida Avenue.

"I had trouble being taken seriously," she said. "There weren't that many black women in real estate in those days." But, she stood her ground, and gradually established the all-important contacts with banks, title companies, and other financial institutions. Her first years, she said, were spent trying to cut through the tangle of legal, institutional, and social restrictions in an effort to find homes for her largely black clientele.

She returned to Howard to finish the work for her B.A. in sociology. Working in Washington real estate during the fifties and sixties was a sociology course in itself, she said, when "blockbusting, red-lining, and credit discrimination" prevailed. She was committed to finding homes for blacks and points with pride to her successes in opening up many areas of the city. "I always tried to move in families who would educate their white neighbors."

Female-headed households have been a special problem and a special challenge to Beatrice Reed. "I didn't care what the red tape said, I talked with the women and sat them down with the project people. I know what a woman can do," she said.

The National Association of Real Estate Brokers (Realtists) (1025 Vermont Avenue, N.W., Washington, D.C., 20005) was formed thirty years ago to represent minorities in the profession at a time when other doors to organized real estate were closed.

"From its inception," said Gladys Chretien, prominent black real estate entrepreneur of Los Angeles, "the fundamental purpose of NAREB was not just to serve the vested interest of its members, but to promote fair housing and equal opportunity in housing. We feel that we know best some of the cities' needs and problems because we have never escaped."

The organization has a predominantly black Women's Council founded by four women, Daisy Donovan of Detroit, Pinky Harris and Laura Seale, both of New York, and Mattye Spivey of Los Angeles. While most black women in real estate are now members of the National Association of Realtors, with some heading boards, they still maintain their membership in NAREB.

## You've come a long way.

Women have come a long way since Hanna Freud risked growing a beard by engaging in sales, Flaxie Pinkett worked at a basement desk, and California jailed Margaret Herbert's broker for embezzlement. They have come from the "boy for rental" era to kitchen and curbstone brokerage; from dusting men's desks and cleaning fly specks off real estate's front windows, to top producers in residential sales. From residential sales, they have moved into every area of the industry—commercial-industrial, farm and land, international sales, investment counseling, appraising, property management, sales management, and general brokerage.

In 1927, a young, pretty Vera Rivers surreptitiously

wrote up a deposit receipt on the hood of a 1925 Ford Roadster, and was paid a commission of $25 on a $6,000 sale. Fifty years later, another pretty, young woman, Rose Marie Garrison, of Atlanta, writes half-million-dollar contracts locating such foreign firms as Boehringer of West Germany; Hitachi, Kantai, Kawasaki and Yashika Inca of Japan in her city; is named a lifetime member of the Industrial Division of Atlanta's Million Dollar Club; and is referred to by her Japanese businessmen clients as "a powerful woman."

Women are not only eating in the private dining room, and off the best china, many are now in leadership positions in the five-hundred-thousand-member National Association of Realtors (the largest trade organization in the world). And, not one man, according to unimpeachable sources, has gone to Hell—for that reason.

# CHAPTER 3

# Residential Sales—
# Bonanza for Women

> *A hundred men make an
> encampment, but it takes a woman to
> make a home.*
> Chinese proverb

*Selling a way of life.*

"If you live on this earth, own a piece of it. The good Lord put the earth here for people to use."

In the late 1940s, two young children in tow, Routh Robbins followed her serviceman husband from Texas to the swollen Virginia suburbs and began the seemingly impossible task of finding a home. Her task accomplished, she began helping other service wives locate. The transition to professional real estate saleswoman was easy; it seemed natural to capitalize on her knowledge of the Washington suburbs, her understanding of housing needs, and her military ties.

Thirty years later, Routh Robbins's fourteen-office real estate empire employed three to four thousand people and did an annual business of $150 to $160 million in residential sales. If she talked more of her two

children and eight grandchildren than of her accomplishments in the business world, it somehow did
not seem unnatural—for like all successful women in
residential sales she sold more than homes. She sold a
way of life.

A Texas broker recalls that he once ran an office in
which there were no women and was firmly resolved
that there would never be any women in his office. He
now believes that a broker who discriminates against
women is either inexperienced or a misanthrope who is
not especially interested in making money. It would be
difficult to find such a man in today's real estate market.
With women now responsible for an approximate 70
percent of all residential property sales in the United
States, promising new licensees are courted, and proven
producers persuaded to change firms with the offer of a
better commission split. Some brokers finance the training and licensing of likely producers.

"Is there some strange rapport that surfaces between
two women when they're talking 'nests'?" a male broker
wondered.

Perhaps. And perhaps the rapport stems from the fact
that most women are inherently "nesters." Nesting
fever has been known to strike a girl down as early as age
nine, and scientists have observed symptoms in women
past ninety. Most males come equipped with a built-in
immunity to the ravages of the disease.

One out of every five families in the nation changes
addresses each year, and according to Alice Bowman,
home-moving consultant, it is the woman who is most
affected by the move.

"The wife and mother has the most difficult role to
play," she said, explaining that it is she who is usually
responsible for the handling of the move because the
husband has already gone ahead. "Getting out of one

home and into another is both a physical and emotional burden on a woman," she added.

The typical Mary Mover on the front seat of an agent's sedan, her children on the rear seat in their last clean pair of underpants, is a pitiable creature. An agent (spelled nester) who has pulled her own children up by the roots, watched her own couch and hotcake turner disappear in the direction of U.S. 66, and backed the family station wagon down the driveway because her husband has gone ahead, is able to identify with her client's suicidal thoughts.

"It's the little things you do for a woman in this difficult time that count," successful broker Sue Schaeffer of Marin County, California, said. "Telling her about the cleaner who won't shrink her good knits, a dependable alteration woman, the activities available for her children—a list of babysitters, and the name of a doctor.

"Men sometimes bring an expensive plant on the day the buyers move into their new home. But I suggest a hot casserole. That woman is probably too tired to get dressed—much less see that three or four children are presentable enough to enter a restaurant. And there's *nothing,*" she emphasized, "so discouraging as the sight of cold lunchmeat and a loaf of bread on a dish-stacked unfamiliar drainboard."

Sue speaks with authority. The wife of a retired military officer, she moved "in" and subsequently "out" of fifteen nests in twenty-three years.

For whatever reason—empathy, know-how, desire to please, willingness to work a little harder—the success of women in the sale of residential property is unprecedented in American business lore.

Ebby Halliday of Dallas, Texas, has sold a house a day for twenty-five years. In annual volume, the Halliday organization is the largest wholly owned residential real estate company in the world.

In 1945, Ebby was a millinery buyer for a Dallas department store. Persuaded to help a friend sell fifty-two revolutionary concrete-block houses that weren't moving, she decorated three of them—creating some of the first model homes in the business. All fifty-two homes sold readily. She was in real estate.

Her nine-office, two-hundred-associate firm has a full-time training director and stays in the forefront of new innovations. Executive Vice-President Paul Hanson works with corporations on their transfer requirements and travels the country training people in other firms in this specialized service.

Ebby was one of three founders of the Inter-City Relocation Service, a computer program now joined by top member firms throughout the world. An ICRS member may sell (or lease) the home of a family in one city and speed the location of a suitable home for the family in another city. Ebby predicts that the system will continue to grow on a nationwide basis until one day the property in every township, county, city, and state can be made available to every Realtor in America.

The Halliday service is world-wide. Dallas draws newcomers from Europe and other continents, she explains, and they have the same problems of a moving American corporate executive—plus many more. Expertise in handling the special needs of people from foreign countries has earned her a place on the board of the American Chapter of the International Real Estate Federation.

The *Honolulu Star Bulletin* on an April Sunday advertised nine properties for sale by Myra Fisher Incorporated:

"Noela Drive—Diamond Head, $950,000"
"Noela Drive—newly constructed, $950,000"
"Kaneohe Bay Drive—$350,000"

"On the ocean at Diamond Head—apartment home, $265,000"

"Coral Strand—2 bedroom 2 bath apartment, $179,000"

"On the ocean at Wailupe Peninsula—$325,000"

"Villa Penthouse—$350,000"

"Waikiki Place golf course—$180,000"

"Noela Drive—Diamond Head, $400,000"

Widowed in the early fifties, Myra opened a hotel apartment booking agency in Honolulu. Booking a client into a private home on Kahala Beach instead of into an apartment hotel elicited a visit from a representative of the Real Estate Commission, who informed her that she was engaging in the real estate profession without a license.

After receiving her broker's license in 1955, she helped open the first real estate office in Waikiki for the Bishop Trust Company in the glamorous Princess Kaiulani Hotel. By 1959, she had her own company, "Land Investments," on Kalakaua Avenue in Waikiki, and was employing fourteen salespeople.

In 1962 she took a trip around the world, talking to real estate boards in Rome, Manila, and Tokyo, and "decided that there were other places to live than Honolulu. Maybe not as beautiful, but more exciting."

The following year she moved to New York City, received her broker's license and joined a Madison Avenue firm. In 1964, Previews International requested that she come to London for the purpose of selling Grand Bahamas Island. Upon completion of her London work, she accepted a position with Tishman Realty and Construction Company as director of advertising and public relations of their West Coast headquarters in Los Angeles. Obtaining her California broker's license, she did the public relations work for the Wilshire Sheraton

Hotel, then became sales manager for the Wilshire Comstock. Upon her return to Honolulu in 1968, she was hired as leasing agent for the Financial Plaza, and subsequently by one of the tenants, Grosvenor International of London.

In 1973, she opened her own office, Myra Fisher Incorporated, in Honolulu, handling "not expensive, as the public calls it," she said, "but interesting properties from $150,000 to $1,000,000." She recently handled the subdivision of a four-acre estate on the ocean at Diamond Head (with the assistance of twenty-six-year-old daughter, Lindy). Lots were priced from $260,000 to $540,000. All sold in six months, purchased primarily by land developers for private home sites. "They knew the value and acted quickly," she said. Myra now divides her time between her Honolulu home and a recently purchased apartment on Nob Hill in San Francisco.

Poised Gertrude Abbott typifies the mature, successful residential agent. She has sold close to $30 million worth of residential real estate in the past ten years, and now manages one of Northern California's most productive residential offices. The fourteen sales agents under her supervision are all women. Nine of them, including Mrs. Abbott, sold $1 million or more of housing property in 1975. White-haired grandmother Evelyn Morgan posted sales of $3,211,000 in 1975, the highest noncommercial sales figure ever recorded by the Sacramento Board of Realtors for a member associate.

### The two essential factors for success in residential sales.

They are (1) recognizing the worth of your product, and (2) recognizing your own worth.

1. *The product.* The word "home" has perhaps as deep a meaning as any in our language. It is a structure, a thing of boards and bricks, affording shelter. It is the first and the most important investment made by most Americans.

Payments on a mortgage mean that the buyer is acquiring a major possession, and the improvements made not only enhance a way of life, they increase the value of the home.

Taxes on the home and the interest on the mortgage are deductible from income tax.

Home ownership makes one a part of a community and establishes a credit rating.

Children grow up in the neighborhood of the parents' choice, and equity built up in a home is usually better than a savings account since it can appreciate to keep pace with inflation.

2. *The competent agent.* Do they need you to sell their home? The answer is a resounding "yes." Put more succinctly by peppery octogenarian—and top producer—Margaret Herbert of Beverly Hills, "People who try to sell their own homes have a fool for a client! And it's dangerous, with all the nuts running around these days."

"Do you act as your own physician? Your own tax accountant? Your own attorney?" asks Sandy Augliere, president of Barcroft Properties, Inc., of Arlington, Virginia.

"For most people, the answer is 'No.' It should be 'No' in handling what may well be the biggest monetary transaction of your life."

## Location.

Industry lore holds that the three most important factors in the value of a home are (1) location, (2) location, and (3) location; for even the most attractive home, built with the finest of materials, must be in a desirable residential atmosphere if its value is to appreciate. One of the most important services an agent brings to a buyer is the determination and evaluation of all factors affecting the location of various properties. Since location means different things to different people, the competent agent points out to clients they must evaluate location in terms of their own present and future needs, must recognize that location means more than the physical site of their home, that it includes the neighborhood, community facilities, people, and regulations that go along with the site.

If schools are important, how far away are they? Can the children walk or must they take a bus? How far is it to shopping? How far to their place of employment? Is commuting available? What churches and medical facilities are nearby?

What are the taxes apt to be? How much does insurance cost in a particular location?

Is the property near a flight path, major highway, or railroad whose noise might disturb them? Are there nearby factories that produce noise, smoke, and traffic? Is the location particularly windy?

Is the lot big enough? If they plan on expanding the home later, is there enough space? Is the exposure to sunlight right for their needs? This may be important if they want a garden or expect to grow house plants. Is the view what they'd like?

Can they park their car on the street overnight? Are they allowed to put up a fence? Can they keep a boat in their driveway? What are the restrictions on remodeling and room additions? Are there commercial or industrial buildings nearby—or apt to be?

Is the site in an incorporated or unincorporated area? How are police and fire protection provided? What about the water supply and waste disposal? Are they in a special taxing district? If the streets are not paved, will they have to pay a special assessment for paving later on? Are the sewers adequate in the area?

## Pricing.

A realistic selling price is perhaps the most important service an agent brings to a seller client, for just as the finest workmanship cannot sell a house in the wrong location, the finest advertising and sales efforts cannot sell a home unless the price is right. Prospective buyers shy away from a home out of their price range, and when the price is eventually reduced to a realistic figure, the public may recall the length of time the property has been on the market and draw the conclusion that there's something wrong with the home itself—or perhaps the neighborhood. There is a misconception that a purchaser pays more for property when it is listed with a broker because the seller has to pay the commission and has added it on to the price. A study of "For Sale by Owner" signs will show evidence that the owner-seller has usually priced his home to the "asking price" of others in the neighborhood, rather than the actual "selling price." This is understandable, for without the multiple listing service cumulative index of sales of all properties with the same tax key section and zone number, the owner has little information to draw on—other than the classified section of the newspaper and word of mouth.

A resale home on Oscar Owner's street (same floor plan as Oscar's) was advertised for $46,000, and sold within a month. Another priced at $45,000 sold within six weeks. Since his wife, Opal, had redecorated their home by installing wall-to-wall blue carpeting, and papering their eight-year-old daughter's room in a blue and pink floral, Oscar tacked $2,000 onto the $46,000 price and advertised his home for $48,000. And advertised. And advertised. And advertised.

Advertising can be a very expensive hobby for the amateur. While few would agree with Aldous Huxley that "it is far easier to write ten possibly effective sonnets, good enough to take in the not too inquiring critic, than one effective advertisement that will take in a few thousand of the uncritical buying public," few would disagree that writing an eye-catching ad takes imagination and skill. Most prospects do not buy the advertised home about which they inquire, but the professional's advertising money is not wasted, since she or he has other properties to show. Unfortunately, Oscar Owner does not.

A good agent would have advised Oscar that statistics reveal that Opal's planned wall-to-wall expanse of blue carpeting would turn a high percentage of buyers away, and that it would be wise to leave the frayed beige carpet in and make an allowance on the selling price— enabling the buyer to choose a color. While blue and pink floral paper might delight the Owner's eight-year-old daughter, it would not appeal to most buyers.

Referring to the multiple listing service cumulative index, the agent would have revealed to Opal and Oscar that one of the houses used as a pricing guideline brought $43,500, and the other $44,000, and that the cumulative index showed similar homes in the neighborhood selling in that range.

Oscar and Opal Owner had priced their home approximately $4,000 above fair market value for the area. The conscientious agent in talking to a prospective listing owner offers to make a market value study but never uses the word appraisal. The market valuation made by a broker or agent falls far short of the scientific data study and computations made by a qualified appraiser. If suitable comparables cannot be found to supply an owner a fair market value price by searching the cumulative index of the multiple listing service, they can sometimes be located by checking the local recorder's office to determine the amount of transfer taxes paid on each separate piece of property in the area. Sometimes such tax is levied only on the equity transferred, not on the full sales price. Another method is to look up the documents recorded with the transfer of each separate piece of property. The mortgage or trust deed amount is often recorded.

But pricing property to sell involves more than just comparing it with other similar properties recently sold. The uniqueness of each property and its own values are based on location, condition, financing, amenities, and other marketing factors. There is no exact price on any property, but there is a range in values that are influenced by other marketing considerations. Only the professional has the training and tools to arrive at a figure beneficial to the client.

Oscar and Opal Owner, attempting to sell their own home, are literally married to the property—waiting for the phone to ring or for someone to drive by and knock on the door. Even Opal's trips to the grocery store, while Oscar is away at work, put them temporarily out of business. And it is virtually impossible for them to protect themselves against nonproductive involvements. Their FOR SALE BY OWNER sign is an open invitation, and it is difficult if not impossible for them to question visitors' motivations.

The professional agent qualifies a prospect and finds

what the buyer needs and wants before showing property, so that only those who *should* be inside Oscar and Opal's home ever gain access to it. Once inside, the agent uses that knowledge to show prospective buyers how the house fits their needs.

A likely buyer, seeing Oscar and Opal's sign, and stopping in for an unannounced guided tour of the premises, is literally on his own once he leaves the embarrassed Opal. There is no agent to influence him, to perceive and point out the values in the property that have nothing to do with the diapers on the bathroom floor. The prospective buyer must form his own judgment as to the value of the home.

## Preparing the home for sale.

The professional is aware that small details make strong first impressions, and would have advised Oscar and Opal to fix that sticking closet door, oil that squeaking hinge, and put a washer in that leaky faucet. All of these, and a dozen other minor defects can aggravate potential buyers and sometimes impede a sale.

Attractive, articulate Mandy Ahlstrand is a director of the Boulder, Colorado, Board of Realtors and president of Women's Council for Colorado. Mandy's real estate roots go deep. Her grandfather entered the profession in New York in 1890, her mother sold property in Florida from 1952 to 1965, and an uncle was the negotiating broker for the land on which the United Nations Building now stands. Mandy's special area of interest is residential sales, and she conducts seminars on the subject. Here are some of the points she made on preparing a house for showing.

"Clients should be advised that a few dollars spent on cleaning and painting not only makes their home more attractive but frequently makes it easier to get their asking price.

"In addition to being sparkling clean, a house should have a nice aroma. A pot of water on the back of the stove with a cinnamon stick in it is a good idea. Towels should be fresh and neatly arranged. Bars of soap should be clean. All drapes and sheers should be open (unless you have an unsightly view from a window). All lights should be on."

The competent agent will discourage a practice which may have cost Oscar and Opal a sale, the bringing along of friends.

"Encourage your prospective buyers to ask for outside expertise in evaluating such things as wiring, plumbing, etc.," she said, "but discourage them from bringing along friends to view the house.

"It is important that the grounds be presentable, no leaves, weeds, or toys strewn about. And no dogs!" she emphasized.

It is the rare prospective buyer who appreciates being backed against the garage wall by a fang-bared, drooling German shepherd or having a French poodle jump to her lap and lick the powder from her nose.

## Finance.

Financing is frequently the key to residential sales. The competent real estate professional explains to both parties that real estate financing for homes is essentially based on the qualifications of the property, the buyers, the type of home, and current mortgage market conditions and that, primarily, home loans can be classified in three broad categories: (1) conventional loans (uninsured or insured), (2) government insured or assisted loans, and (3) private financing.

A client's ability to qualify and to pay the best real estate loan depends upon his or her total financial picture and how it is documented and presented to the lending institution. The professional knows that there are many ways that a buyer's position may be improved when assembling a financing package for a lender, taking into account the major factors of buyer's total assets, total liabilities, credit history, annual family income, employment history, and security.

Points or loan fees charged for initiating new financing are confusing and often cause contention between buyer and seller. The competent agent can sometimes avoid the cancellation of a sale by explaining to both buyer and seller that such costs result from the mortgage lender's need to compensate for the differences in mortgage interest rates and the current market value or cost of long-term money. Usury laws, government rulings on federally insured loans, and other factors determine how many points or costs can be levied or who can pay them.

Prepayment privileges are another important consideration for a client, and conventional loans can vary greatly in this matter. The right to pay off the loan prior to the maturity date frequently involves additional costs, and the professional verifies this aspect before closing the loan, especially if the client anticipates early resale or refinancing.

The client selling one home in order to buy another is in need of special assistance in arranging an interim or bridge loan. Such equity financing can be made available by the seller of the property being purchased, by the client's own bank, or in some cases by the real estate broker. A guarantee on the seller's equity is sometimes a practical method. Some firms offer a "guaranteed sales plan," a commitment that if the property is not sold on or before a specific date the guaranteeing party will purchase the property for a net amount agreed upon in advance. In the meantime, the property is marketed at its current value in an attempt to secure a price in excess of the guarantee. The counseling that the professional must do in financing begins with taking the listing, continues in working with a buyer on the phrasing of his offer, figures prominently in presenting the offer to the seller for acceptance, and ends when the offer is accepted and the actual loan is arranged.

Your expertise in the above areas, your ability to locate buyers, communicate with both buyer and seller, write and place ads, write a good "fool-proof" contract, and choose the most propitious moment to close the transaction, make you, the residential agent, one of the most outstanding values in the United States today.

## Choosing the right broker.

In most companies the agent is not an employee but an independent contractor, with her earnings entirely dependent on commissions and with few fringe benefits. For this reason, an important step toward a successful career is choosing the right broker. Mary Shern who has capped twenty-five years of success in real estate as agent, broker, and developer by establishing the Mary Shern School of Real Estate in Honolulu believes that the beginner should ask herself the following six questions:

1. Would I be proud to be associated with this broker?
2. Is he active in the area where I want to work and in the field that interests me?
3. What does he offer me in training and continuing education?

4. Is his advertising impressive, both in quantity and quality?

5. Does his plan for commission-sharing seem fair in comparison with other firms?

6. Do the people in this company seem congenial?

Of the six requirements listed, number (3) should be considered imperative.

Successful black broker Daisy Donovan of Detroit, a leader in organized real estate, lists training and education as the two essentials a beginning agent must look for when selecting a broker. "If he doesn't offer you training and education, you're simply donating your time to him," she said emphatically.

Doris McRoberts serves as training director for the highly successful American Marketing and Development Corporation of Sacramento.

"Must your agents complete their six weeks course in training before they're allowed to sell?" I asked.

"They can sell—but they're always with a seasoned agent. We don't want them to go out alone—not to show a house, or list a house. We don't even want them on floor duty without an experienced agent at their side.

"We want them to learn to 'work smart.' "

Suppose you make a mistake—put your license with the wrong firm! Suppose you find that there is a lack of training, a paucity of advertising—but a flourishing game of "throw the business" to a female agent in return for the throwing of favors more commonly associated with the bedroom than the office? Will you suffer in silence (spelled poverty) for fear of becoming a firm hopper? Your answer is "Yes"? Have you thought of addressing envelopes at home in your spare time? A woman in Albany, New York, made enough to buy a new typewriter after only two years in the business.

Graduation from training bra.

Some women suggest that the new agent call on everyone from whom she has purchased something, or with whom she has done business—service station attendants, dry cleaners, grocery store checkers, pharmacists, furniture store salespeople, car dealers, doctors, dentists, barbers, beauticians, and insurance agents.

"Drive through a different neighborhood every day."

"Call two 'for-sale-by-owners' every week."

"Mail ten letters soliciting new business every week."

"Call on builders, officers of savings and loan associations or banks and attorneys," San Rafael, California, Realtor Jane Fairchild advised. "PTA, Scouts, and Little League can be excellent sources of business."

Knowing that she cannot be totally familiar with all the available houses in a city, the wise beginning agent selects a portion of the city to work and learns her territory thoroughly—the school zones, recreation areas, nearest shopping areas, nearest available transportation, recent sales in the area, and actual selling prices.

In addition to familiarizing herself with the needs of her clients, she must also be familiar with all available listings in her area—other firms as well as her own. "She should know room sizes, workmanship of buildings, and lot sizes," said Basalle Wong, who sold thirty-two houses in San Francisco's Sunset district during a period of six months in 1965—her first year in the business.

"Be community oriented," said petite Beatrice Reed, a past president of the Washington (D.C.) National Association of Real Estate Brokers. "I'm committed to finding homes for blacks and lower income families.

And I try to secure loans to rehabilitate urban properties."

"Self-starter," "self-motivated," "self-disciplined"—these three phrases bob to the surface most frequently in every discussion of the prerequisites for success.

Some people in the industry are convinced that the phenomenal success of women in residential sales results from hard work rather than some magic rapport between women. Gertrude Abbott, of Sacramento, speaking of the fourteen outstandingly successful women under her supervision, said, "Each salesperson in the office is allowed one month a year off, but nobody takes any more than two weeks in actual vacation time. The office is open seven days a week, and most saleswomen are here sometime during every day. Or at least they check in by telephone.

"Many of them begin their phone calls at 6:30 or 7:00 in the morning and they are often out as late as 11:00 or midnight if an offer or counter-offer for property is pending."

Routh Robbins believes that women do the lion's share of business in residential sales because they feel "at home" in a suburban setting. "Women are the ones who live in the suburbs," she said, "and women are the ones who know how to sell them."

Joan Thomas of the all-female Nancy Reynolds and Associates firm of Westfield, New Jersey, credits "luck, savvy, and drudgery" for her success.

Certainly luck was on Cynthia Bell's side in Honolulu, when one week after she received her real estate license, a wealthy client came through the door looking for an estate-type property on Oahu. Nothing on the market pleased him. Cynthia heard that the Kaiser estate might be available, contacted the owners, listed the property for $2 million, sold it, and collected lister and seller commissions—3 percent of $2 million!

Real estate agent Antoinette Hatfield, wife of United States Senator Mark Hatfield, recently sold Saudi Arabian Ambassador Ali Alireza a new official residence in Washington for about $1 million; Sadie Clark sells homes in the $15,000 to $25,000 bracket in a Los Angeles ghetto area. Mary Shern of Honolulu began her career in real estate with a degree in economics; Lydia Franz of Illinois with a master's; while Basalle Wong began her real estate career without a high school diploma. One agent took off her cap and gown and came in at twenty-two; another untied her apron and came in at sixty-two. In spite of disparate backgrounds, these women have one thing in common—*success.*

In their study of over seventy-thousand real estate sales and management personnel, Herbert and Jeanne Greenberg of Marketing Survey and Research found that experience and education were "two of the most used (or perhaps abused) criteria" for success in real estate. People without even a high school diploma performed as well as people with advanced degrees, the Greenbergs' study showed. People with no previous real estate or even sales experience performed as well as a group as those coming into a company with a substantial real estate background. Stereotyped notions to the contrary, people over forty produced as effectively as their younger competitors. And the trait pattern of the middle-class black groups proved to be nearly identical to that of white applicants.

What counts? What is important?

According to the Greenbergs: "*The dynamics within a human being.*"

# CHAPTER 4

## Four Keys to Success. How to Make Them Work for You.

*Money is everything. If you don't believe it–ask the woman who hasn't any.*
Ancient American female adage

Do your clients talk so much they are unable to hear you?

Is your approach to qualifying a prospective buyer: "How much money do you make?"

Do you feel that the details of going to escrow deserve the same privacy as going to the bathroom, and discussion of either has no place between buyer and sales agent?

Does the idea of saving a client some money leave you as uninterested as last February's weather report? Questioning: "Has that client ever tried to save me any money?" Answering: "Not one damn cent!"

If your answer is "yes" to the above questions, you need not consult your horoscope, your favorite seer, or your palm to learn that: "You will meet many people." "You will see the inside of many homes." "You will have a successful career as an unpaid chauffeur."

Interviews with agents, brokers, sales managers, escrow officers, and unhappy principals reveal that four categories—failure to qualify prospects properly, inability to communicate effectively, inept performances in the drama of escrow, and a total disregard for the elusive art of saving both buyer and seller money—send many women to the photographer for their appointment for real estate's dropout album.

## Qualifying.

CONSEQUENCES OF SHOWING THE $40,000 HOUSE
TO THE $30,000 POCKETBOOK.

"She spent two weeks showing my wife and me property we discovered at the last minute was too damn expensive!" an irate first-time would-be-buyer said. "She wasted our time—and her gas!"

Failure to qualify prospects before showing homes is a major public relations problem plaguing the industry. Despite its obvious necessity, some agents tend to ignore it. As a result the entire industry suffers loss of public esteem.

Connie Reade Client Relations, a Fresh Meadows, New York, firm, conducts an annual survey of 150,000 families who have recently purchased homes to determine their opinion of the real estate firm serving them. Though the survey is conducted among customers of the industry's more progressive brokerage offices, the last survey indicated that over 32 percent rated the service they received as fair or poor. Buyers who responded negatively were displeased with vague cost estimates, inaccurate tax figures, viewing homes out of their reach, and blurry financing requirements.

"According to our survey," Arthur Kaye, a principal in the company said, "too many associates are not spending that thirty or forty minutes creating an empathy with the prospect by discovering his needs and wants. Instead, they have him out looking at houses five minutes after he enters the office. They show him what he wants without being realistic enough to realize that the prospect will probably wind up settling for what he needs.

"The surprise comes," according to Kaye, "when suddenly the agent discloses his well-kept secret of closing costs, monthly carrying charges, etc. Even if the prospect goes through with the deal, he loses respect for the salesperson. In reviewing questionnaires received from buyers who rated their real estate firm as good or excellent, we find they consider time spent in the office prior to home inspections a professional approach."

The Berg Agency, with eighteen offices in New Jersey, discovered how great the problem was when a local survey revealed that as many as 35 percent of prospective buyers are turned down when they apply for a mortgage. According to Jerry Salomone, president of the company, "Part of the problem is that home buyers are not being properly counseled. If a customer's income is not high enough for his personal 'dream house,' he should be encouraged to settle for a smaller dwelling that will at least give him ownership status. When his income rises, and hopefully his first home appreciates, he can trade up."

## WHAT DO THEY WANT? WHAT CAN THEY AFFORD?

The decision as to what type of property to show a particular prospect rests on these two basic questions. But beware of judging by appearances! Clothes may make the man—or woman—but they do not necessarily make the qualified buyer of real estate. The industry is rife with stories of little old ladies who, upon deciding on a property, excused themselves, stepped into the ladies room, reached into their Supphose, and came out carrying thirty or forty thousand dollars in bills of various denominations.

Students of the Mary Shern School of Real Estate in Honolulu are advised to ask direct, pertinent—yet diplomatic—questions when qualifying prospects. "How much would you *like* to pay down?" or "How much of your savings would you like to liquidate as the initial investment in your home?" rather than the bald, "How much *can* you put down?"

If a prospect's down payment appears inadequate, they are counseled to consider whether it can be supplemented. Does the prospect own other real estate with the possibility of refinancing or a blanket mortgage? Does the prospect own stocks and bonds which may be sold or pledged? Does the prospect have life insurance with a borrowing capacity? Are there relatives willing to help with a noninterest or low-interest loan?

The rule that a monthly payment, including taxes, principal, interest, and insurance should not be more than one-fourth the family's monthly income should be measured against number of dependents, type of employment, future career prospects, existing indebtedness, possibility of mortgage cosigner, and life-style.

Marilyn Boening of Pittsburgh taught real estate sales at Pennsylvania State University for four years, is a faculty member of the Pennsylvania Realtors Institute, and a much-in-demand speaker at seminars and conventions nationwide. As director of training and public relations for the Pittsburgh firm of Benson & Sons, Marilyn devised a Prospect Profile form covering the essential aspects of buyer's circumstances, specifications, and finances. The form Marilyn sent me serves as a reminder to agents to ask all pertinent questions and provides a permanent record of the prospect's answers.

After gaining permission to ask personal questions, agents fill out the form shown on page 65. The "work sheet" portion of the form (lower left corner) records the information necessary to establish an accurate price range for the buyer.

## Communicating.

The greatest problem of communication, according to George Bernard Shaw, is the illusion that it has been accomplished.

Are you "taking turns talking" to your clients?

"A woman begins a sale by selling herself," said highly successful Gladys Chretien of Los Angeles.

She warns her salespeople, she said, that selling is not an assemblyline operation. "There is no standard formula for handling people. What pleases one person may irritate another. The woman who thinks she can handle every client in the same manner is going to have a mediocre career."

"No matter how knowledgeable and efficient?" I asked.

"And no matter how thoughtful and pleasant," she said.

Communication has been defined as giving to another person. Transmitting. Imparting. Joining. It is the art of interchanging thoughts, opinions, and information by voice, eyes, appearance, body language.

What is the secret to acquiring that magic capacity to recognize clues and cues thrown out by others? How does a woman acquire the ability to get feedback from clients so that she can adjust her behavior and sales talk to their individual needs and desires?

A giant step in the right direction according to Gladys and several other successful women is: Listen. Listen. Listen.

ANALYSIS OF HOME OWNERSHIP COSTS

(For Taxpayer Using Itemized Deductions)

PREPARED FOR: <u>Mr. Prospect</u>     THE COUNTRY SQUIRE, REALTORS

By: <u>Mr. Associate</u>

1. Sale Price of Home:                          <u>$50,000.00</u>

2. Cash Required:        <u>$ 10,000.00</u>

3. Loan:                 <u>$ 40,000.00</u>

4. Monthly Payments, principal and interest:    $    335.69

5. Monthly Deposit for taxes, approximately:    $     85.00

6. Monthly Deposit for insurance, approximately: <u>$    15.00</u>

7. TOTAL MONTHLY PAYMENT:                        $    435.69

8. EXPENSE ITEMS FOR INCOME TAX PURPOSES:

9. First month interest:      <u>$   300.00</u>

10. Monthly tax deposit:      <u>$    85.00</u>

11. TOTAL DEDUCTIONS:         $   385.00

*(12.) In 50% tax bracket, deduct cash saving per month: <u>$ 192.50</u>

(13.) In 40% tax bracket, deduct cash saving per month: <u>$ 154.00</u>

(14.) In 30% tax bracket, deduct cash saving per month: <u>$ 115.50</u>

(15.) In 20% tax bracket, deduct cash saving per month: <u>$  77.00</u>
       *To calculate, multiply tax bracket by "TOTAL DEDUCTIONS" on Line 11.

16. Total Monthly Payment:  (Line 7)                     <u>$ 435.69</u>

17. Subtract Applicable Deduction (Line 12, 13, 14, or 15) <u>$ 115.50</u>

18. ACTUAL MONTHLY <u>PAYMENT</u>:                            <u>$ 320.19</u>

19. Subtract EQUITY which is being gained monthly:       <u>$  35.69</u>
                     (Line 4 minus Line 9)

20. ACTUAL MONTHLY <u>COST</u>:                               <u>$ 284.50</u>

---

Interest decreases by small amount each month,
but equity increases by the same amount.

"And analyze what you're hearing," said Gladys. "How does that man or woman really feel? What does he really want? What is most important to her, prestige or comfort? *And what does he mean besides what he is saying?*"

The proliferation of courses in colleges and universities, as well as the introduction of training programs by American business firms, should alert every woman to the importance of acquiring the ability to communicate effectively.

THE TELEPHONE. THE ALL-IMPORTANT TOOL
OF YOUR TRADE.

The wise real estate professional is aware that her voice and manner when handling telephone calls may very well determine the degree of her success.

"That first call from a prospective buyer or seller is the most important one you'll take," said Maxine DeBoer of Anchorage, Alaska. "Your voice must immediately convey professionalism and a desire to help."

She pointed out that the telephone is of particular importance in such areas as Alaska. "Of necessity so much of our contact is by phone. Properties can be hundreds or thousands of miles away, accessible only by air.

"When you meet a client in person you have any number of ways to establish rapport, or good communication. Your eyes. A warm smile. Body language. But when you meet him for the first time on the phone, as we often do here, you have only your voice going for you. Your voice must inspire confidence in your ability to handle the caller's business, or it ends right there. You don't get the listing. He doesn't make an appointment.

"What you say," she ended, "is sometimes less important than how you say it."

Maxine came to Alaska during World War II and has

never had any desire, she said, to return to the "Lower 48." "Alaska is not a place. It's a way of life. Everything is exciting here, and real estate is one of the most exciting things about this state."

HOW'S YOUR TELEPHONE TECHNIQUE?
ELEVEN QUESTIONS.

The following eleven questions were designed to test your competence in handling real estate's most important tool.

1. Is it a waste of time to identify your firm or yourself when answering the phone?

2. Is it unnecessary to take messages—since the caller will probably call back anyway?

3. After wringing the caller's name from him, is your next question: "What do you want?"

4. Do you leave the caller hanging while you look up the information on several homes because: "After all, I'd just have to call him back."

5. Do you save time by carrying on a conversation with Mary Agent at the next desk while talking to someone on the phone because: "After all, he probably has no intention of buying a damn thing."

6. Do you let the phone ring three or four times before answering, so the caller will "worry" whether there's anyone in the office?

7. Do you talk on the phone with: (a) cigarette in your mouth? (b) gum? (c) pencil? (d) all of the above?

8. When interrupted by a call which should have been directed to someone else, do you hang up instead of transferring the caller because, "the receptionist should have had better sense?"

9. Do you interrupt a prospective buyer in mid-sentence when you have something important to tell him?

10. Do you ask the agent at the next desk to place a

call to a client for you because you have to call home and tell the kids what to put on for dinner?

11. Do you encourage your seven-year-old to answer an 11:00 A.M. residenc call and explain that: "Mommy's still in bed?" Your seventeen-year-old to show an interest in your clients with: "Oh! Are you the ones who can't get a loan?"

Your answer was "no" to all eleven questions? Turn to the next section.

Your answer was "no" to five questions, "yes" to six? Run—don't walk—to your neighborhood psychiatrist.

You scored "yes" on eleven out of eleven? Rip out your telephone.

SUGGESTIONS ON THE ELUSIVE ART OF COMMUNICATING EFFECTIVELY (gleaned from interviews with successful women throughout the country).

"Key your language to your audience: Use the client's vocabulary. Speak in terms of the client's interests."

"Establish rapport with your client. People communicate best when they are at ease with each other."

"Answer all questions asked by clients—only then, attempt to arouse interest and desire with your own questions."

"*Never* allow children to pick up your residence phone."

"Instruct your family or your answering service to answer client calls with the explanation that you are working with a client, and that they will try to reach you."

(Whether you're under the dryer, attending a PTA meeting, or in a motel room is not the business of the client. If you're doing a good job, he'll wait for your call.)

"Be explicit. Never ambiguous. Don't force a client to

search through a mouthful of rhetoric for your message."

"In answering ad calls—get the caller's name, write it down, and use it. *Use it! Use it!*"

"Match your speed of talking to that of the client, whether in personal or telephone contact. His speed of talking may be a clue to how fast he hears, and absorbs the information you're giving him. If he's a slow and deliberate speaker, slow down. This helps to avoid the impression of high-pressure salesmanship."

(If, on the other hand, his words are ricocheting off your eardrums like bullets, speed it up. But not to the extent that you trip over your tongue, mispronounce his name for the fifth time, tell him to meet you at two when you meant to say four, and give him directions to a rival's office.)

SUMMING IT UP.

Watch the client's response: A slightly dazed look? A sudden interest in a blank wall? Shifting in the seat as if it were covered with horsehair rather than Naugahyde? Legs crossed and recrossed as if in the final stages of terminal poison ivy? Place your license on inactive status and enroll in a course in communication in your nearest university.

## Going to escrow.

The successful agent takes the mystery out of the trip to escrow by explaining the advantages to her clients and assuring them that the escrow procedure exists for the protection of all parties to a real estate transaction. Escrow officers serve as licensed, impartial "stakeholders" and have an exacting job and an awesome responsibility.

Based on contract instructions, the escrow officer: orders title insurance policy, receives loan documents and funds for the buyer, receives buyer's funds, prepares and/or receives deed and other common documents related to escrow, prorates taxes, rents, insurance, etc. The escrow officer you choose to handle your contract also obtains buyer's approval of termite report, records, deeds, and other related documents, disburses payment for title insurance, recording fee, real estate commissions, loan payoffs and other charges as instructed, and prepares a final statement showing uses of monies deposited.

WORDS OF WARNING FROM AN ESCROW OFFICER.

"Some agents think once they've got that deposit slip through, their job is done. Not so. Many deals fall through in escrow." Certified escrow officer Alma Wincapau has been in the business for twenty-five years. In her spare time she delivers lectures on escrow procedures and teaches Escrow I at a northern California college.

"What are some of the common mistakes agents make when writing contracts?"

"Contract changes are not initialed, or the time and date are not noted; buyers' names are not spelled correctly or in full; it is not clear whether buyer will assume the existing insurance or obtain a new policy.

"Sometimes an agent will have to 'eat' part of his or her commission to save a sale, because the contract is written sloppily. Just three words: 'free of charge' cost an agent $500 yesterday. He forgot to add these three words on after 'Buyer to assume impound account.' "

"Assuming the agent has written a good contract,

what can she do to expedite its course through escrow?"

"The agent should check with us at regular intervals to determine what progress has been made. Sometimes they can help us to expedite matters that are delaying the process.

"But, please," she added, "don't waste the escrow agent's time with long or too-frequent calls."

"What about asking a client to call the escrow company to inquire about the contract, if an agent is going to be out of town or is tied up with other business?"

"Never. It's very unprofessional. And agents should avoid asking for rush service, unless it is vital to the contract."

"Anything else?"

"Frequently agents bring clients to the signing without explaining to them that this is not the actual closing, and that no funds will be disbursed until all documents have been recorded after the last signatures have been obtained. There's usually a time lapse of several days.

"Buyers are becoming more educated, and they expect professional service from their agents. The agent who can't deliver it is going to be a loser."

"What's the *single* most important thing an agent can do to assure a smooth functioning escrow process—and avoid losing a contract she's worked on for weeks?"

"Write a good contract!" she said emphatically.

WHY KEEP YOUR BUYERS PUZZLED ABOUT
TITLE INSURANCE?

Since a home represents the largest investment most people make in an entire lifetime, loss of that investment can be tragic. A title insurance policy protects your client against losses from defects in title or ownership in matters of public record as well as hidden defects not found in public records such as: lack of a right of access from the client's land to a public street; taxes or assessments levied by a public authority which constitute liens not shown prior to purchase date; unrecorded liens for labor or material from improvements in progress or completed at the date of the policy unless the insured owner has agreed to be responsible; encroachment of the residential structure or any part of it onto adjoining lands; violations of enforceable covenants, conditions, or restrictions; violations of applicable zoning ordinances and damage to the residential structure resulting from use of surface of the land for extraction or development of minerals.

Some title companies now offer an "appreciation policy" designed to safeguard owners from mounting real estate values. As your client's property increases in value, the amount of ownership insurance coverage also will rise. Percentage increase will be based on the Construction Cost Index of the U.S. Department of Commerce, computed annually.

SEVEN POINTS TO REMEMBER.

A successful escrow closing and final culmination of a sale—resulting in a commission in the four-figure column—begins with a successful opening. Here are some points made by agents, brokers, clients, and escrow officers to guard against the untimely death of a sale in escrow.

1. Advise your seller to provide you with the name, address, zip code, and loan number of the existing lender, if any. Ask for a copy of the grant deed or policy of title insurance—this information will give the title company a base to work from. Ask for details on fire insurance, rental information, if the property is rented, and copies of leases, if any.

2. Ask your buyers upon making an offer to purchase to complete a statement of information. And assure

them that the information is confidential and will be used to eliminate matters of record concerning persons with a same or similar name.

3. Be sure you give all details of the transaction to the escrow officer. Make sure all items are submitted promptly.

4. Ask the escrow officer to send you a copy of the preliminary reports. Then read them carefully!

5. Keep an escrow progress chart, and check with the escrow agent at regular intervals to determine what progress has been made. But *never* ask buyer or seller to call.

6. Keep in close touch with your buyer, informing him of the various stages and an approximate date for closing. Let him know immediately if there are any roadblocks causing a change in date of closing.

7. Review the closing statements and other pertinent papers with your buyer before accompanying him to the "signing" to make sure that no mistakes have been made.

The escrow has closed, titles have changed, deeds have been recorded, funds disbursed—including your four- (five?) figure commission. Do you now forget this client with whom you have shared the intimacies of a bathroom door that would not close, offer, counter offer, counter-counter offer, acceptance, and the trying, tedious days of escrow? Not if you wish to be successful in this highly competitive business!

Contact with your buyers and sellers after sales is vital. Many successful women keep a card file containing pertinent information about each sale, with a card for both buyer and seller. Each party is contacted a few days after closing to see if they have any complaints.

"They're always happy to receive your call, very appreciative," said Agnes Baar of San Francisco.

Most will have no complaints, she said, but for the

buyer or seller with a complaint, serious or trivial, your obvious interest and your help in solving their problem, real or imagined is not forgotten.

"And this business is built on referrals.

"Some companies do nothing to help the agent along this line. Once the sale is closed you're on your own."

By following up after escrow you can build a personal following even if your company does little or nothing to assist you. Your efforts will pay off tenfold if you are affiliated with a company with the same positive approach.

## The neglected art of saving principal's money.

The one essential way is to make prospects aware of the benefits of owning a home!

Homeowners seldom complain if the price tag on other homes gets bigger with each Sunday issue of the real estate section. They know that the value of their home is increasing. Despite inflation, high taxes and mortgage rates, and a confusing economy, home ownership is still the best, safest, and most prudent move your prospective buyer can make.

If you have young people wondering how they, first-time buyers, can buy a home when the "average" price is out of their reach, Marsh Trimble, publisher of *Professional Builder Magazine*, points a way out of the dilemma.

"Normally, young families [first-time buyers] purchase homes at the low end of the scale. Then, as the value of their home increases, they are able to sell at a profit and move up the scale into a larger, more elegant home, probably in a better neighborhood.

"In this way, an owner achieves a rapidly growing net worth, and keeps pace with inflation."

The first down payment discourages many young families and their discouragement or lack of persistence can cost them for the rest of their lives. If your prospect points out the fact that a typical new house today costs about $45,000 and that with the normal down payment and twenty-five-year, 9 percent mortgage, the ultimate cost of the home would be almost $100,000, Marsh Trimble has an answer for that, too. "A renter," he points out, "during the same span would have paid $80,000 for less space and convenience, perhaps, and have only a bundle of rent receipts instead of equity in a home. The homebuyer is protected from constant escalation in housing costs because he pays no more than the original contract price—while rents are increasing from 7 to 20 percent annually.

"At the end of the mortgage period," Mr. Trimble adds, "the homeowner owns his home which then might very well—present trends continuing—have a six-figure value."

It can also be pointed out to young families alarmed by that $100,000 figure that very few families live in the same house for the life of the loan. Most families move every seven years or so, with the normal family having three or four homes during a span of twenty-five or thirty years—presumably each house better than the last.

"Most families," Mr. Trimble counsels, "would be well advised to make most any sacrifice to save enough money for the down payment on a home. The present crucial period of inflation offers no advantage to waiting or gaining time to buy. But once aboard, the buyer can hedge his investment."

Your best advice to young prospects—married or single: Make the move, *now. Somehow!*

Realtor Lydia Franz, president of Century 21–Country Squire Realtors, Barrington, Illinois, has devised a tool to prove to rental prospects that they can't afford to rent even on a short-term basis.

I became interested in Mrs. Franz' idea when I read an article which she wrote for *Real Estate Today*, official publication of the Realtors National Marketing Institute.

"Most people," she said in the article, "are vaguely aware that there are tax benefits in home ownership, but this form tells them how much they save per month."

The form, which Mrs. Franz and I revised for this book (see page 77), gets the message across to prospects that if they rent a house for $450 (approximately the same as the total monthly payment), they are paying $115 every month to Uncle Sam because they're renting instead of buying the house.

Mrs. Franz does not ask the rental prospect his tax bracket because the form will work regardless of the client's bracket.

"After the prospect has studied the savings outlined on the form, he is asked if he would agree that an estimated rate of inflation of at least 5 percent per year is conservative, and when he agrees, applying the 5 percent inflation factor to the $50,000 results in an anticipated value at the end of a year of $52,500. This is another $208.23 per month to be realistically subtracted from line 20, leaving a net of $76.17 per month to buy the house instead of renting it for $450 per month.

"Even considering that his $10,000 down payment is in the house instead of being otherwise invested—and assuming he could safely find an 8 percent return on that amount—that is only $67 per month to be added back into his monthly cost."

It is pointed out to the buyer that he must come up with $435.00 per month—and that he is only being shown how much of that he gets back in one form or another. "But, on that $450 rental, he doesn't get back a dime!"

# PROSPECT PROFILE FORM

*PERMISSION TO ASK PERSONAL QUESTIONS?

NAME _____WIFE _____

ADDRESS _____HOME PHONE _____ BUS. PHONE _____

CHILDREN _____ BOYS _____ AGES _____ GIRLS _____ AGES _____

HOW MANY WILL BE LIVING IN HOME _____ELIGIBLE FOR VA _____

HUSBAND'S OCCUPATION _____EMPLOYER _____ YRS. _____

PREVIOUS EMPLOYMENT _____SALARY _____ OTHER INCOME _____

WIFE'S OCCUPATION _____EMPLOYER _____ YRS. _____

                        MONTHLY    LEASE              SUB-LET
RENT/OWN PRESENT HOME _____ PAYMT. _____EXPIRES _____ PERMITTED _____

MORTGAGE BALANCE _____MORTGAGEE _____

ASSUMABLE MORTGAGE _____TYPE _____ PRESENT EQUITY _____

MUST YOU SELL YOUR PRESENT HOME TO PURCHASE ANOTHER _____ BY WHOM REFERRED _____

HOW MUCH OF YOUR SAVINGS ARE YOU GOING TO INVEST IN DOWN PAYMT. & C. COSTS _____

DIVISION OF FUNDS:  DOWN PAYMENT _____ CLOSING COSTS _____

LOAN PAYMENTS WITH 12 OR MORE MONTHS REMAINING _____

EXPERIENCE IN THE PRESENT MARKET _____ URGENCY _____

HOBBIES, SPECIAL INTERESTS _____

IS APPROVAL OF ANYONE ELSE NECESSARY IN YOUR DECISION _____

| WORK SHEET | NEW HOME |
|---|---|
| TOTAL MONTHLY INCOME _____ | PRICE RANGE _____ |
| LESS MONTHLY LOAN PAYMENTS _____ | STYLE _____ |
| ADJUSTED MONTHLY INC. _____ | BEDRMS. _____ D.R. _____ |
| DIVIDED BY 4 OR 4.5 _____ | FAM. RM. _____ FRPL. _____ BASMT. _____ |
| SUGGESTED MONTHLY PAYMT. _____ | LOT _____ GARAGE _____ |
| LESS TAX/INS. ALLOW. _____ | FURNITURE STYLE _____ |
| MONTHLY PRIN. & INT. _____ | LOCATION _____ |
| MORTGAGE AMOUNT _____ | OTHER _____ |
| PLUS DOWN PAYMENT _____ | *IF WE FIND A HOME THAT MEETS YOUR NEEDS, |
| SUGGESTED PRICE RANGE _____ | ARE YOU IN A POSITION TO MAKE A FAVORABLE DECISION TODAY? |

The form is useful in other ways too, because it dramatically demonstrates a buyer's ability to move up to a higher price bracket.

When negotiating a counter offer, the form can be used to demonstrate to the buyer that paying the higher price is a very small difference per month, after tax, equity, and inflation considerations.

ON DEPRECIATION ALLOWANCES, CAPITAL GAINS,
INSTALLMENT SALES, WRAP-AROUND MORTGAGES.

Many Americans are not acquainted with their government's tax laws, pertaining particularly to the sale of a home. Far too many, according to professionals, are paying more taxes than they should. It is imperative that agents be knowledgeable in this important area. Here are some of the means employed by successful agents concerned with saving their principal's money.

There are now many older clients selling homes worth from $40,000 to $60,000 on the current market, purchased for $15,000 to $20,000 twenty years ago. You can minimize—in some cases eliminate—the tax on such sales by advising your client to sell on a lease with option to purchase after death. This gives your client a down payment and monthly amount for the rest of his or her life. The proceeds received when the option is exercised after death will go to the heirs or to pay estate taxes, and your client will avoid the capital gains tax. Needless to say, the lease option must be carefully drafted so that it will not be classified as a sale by the IRS.

You may want to advise clients over sixty-five to consider an "installment sale" (providing they have lived in the home at least five of the last eight years), thus avoiding any tax on the profit attributable to the original sales price. The tax on the remainder of the profit can be minimized by spreading out the payments they will be receiving. See that the contract is written so the sellers receive less than 30 percent of the sale price in the year of sale. By holding payments from buyer in the year of sale below 30 percent of the selling price, taxes can be spread out over the years your client receives the buyer's payments. They will be maximizing their income from the interest earnings on the mortgage they carry back, and this interest income will more than compensate for the capital gains tax they pay on their profit from the home.

Your seller-clients may want to entertain the idea of a wrap-around mortgage (wraps around the existing mortgage) because their yield will be higher. They will earn the interest differential between the wrap-around mortgage rate and the usually lower rate on the existing first mortgage. Remember to warn clients that a wrap-around mortgage should only be used if that mortgage is not due upon sale of the property.

On the other hand, your buyers should be warned *not* to ask for a wrap-around mortgage. A second mortgage is cheaper for them.

The conscientious (color her successful) agent will explain to buyers that tax planning for the sale of a home begins when the home is purchased because all buying costs are deductible in the sale of a home—even though the sale may be five or ten years after the purchase. Encourage all buyers to keep careful records. Remind seller clients that they may also deduct expenses for permanent improvements—patios, fencing, pools, additions, etc.

Be sure that sellers are aware that it is possible to postpone any tax on profit through the purchase of another home, costing as much or more than the one sold. Under certain conditions there may be actually no tax payment.

Make sure that your buyers are aware of some of the less known tax savings resulting from home ownership—special assessment or benefit taxes used for civic improvements; transfer and recording fees and taxes if part of the home is used for business or rented to tenants; depreciation for any part of the home used for business or rented to tenants and a proportionate share of transfer and recording fees and taxes; the possibility of prepaying and deducting home mortgage interest in advance; deductibility of loan processing fees, or "points," charged on conventional loans; penalty fees and prepayment fees; interest paid on home improvement loans; interest paid on late tax payments, and theft and casualty losses.

Ultimately, your success will depend on what your buyers and sellers think of you. If they are pleased with the service rendered, convinced of your sincerity, thoroughness, and know-how, you will gain their gratitude (spelled referrals). Referrals are the lifeblood of success in real estate. The agent unable to build a successful referral program can be assured of a prominent spot in the dropout album.

CONVERSATION WITH MONA.

Mona was in the process of putting together the final details of a $5,600,000 shopping center and apartment complex she had been working on for over three years when I called for an appointment. Our short, to the point conversation took place over real estate's most important tool.

"What would your advice be to women on the subject of communicating with clients?"

"For God's sake, know what you're talking about. If you don't understand it, how the Hell can *they* understand it?"

"What about qualifying buyers properly before showing properties?"

"Honey, women who think they can shove a couple into their car and show them so many houses they'll buy one because her feet hurt and he has to go to the john are out of this business before the john door closes."

"Do you feel that all agents should explain the intricacies and benefits of escrow to buyers?"

"Explain escrow? There are women trying to sell real estate who think escrow is something the French scrape off the ground and serve with a wine and butter sauce."

"Should the average sales agent explain the various means by which principals can save money— depreciation allowances, capital gains, installment sale, wrap-around mortgages, ded—"

"The average sales agent? Honey, they've got a study out showing that the average female agent made about $6,000 last year. She may think that depreciation is something that happens only to her body and a wrap-around mortgage is something you wear on chilly nights.

"If you're asking me if a woman who wants to make it in this business should be up on all aspects of finance, tax, new laws enacted, bills pending, etc., and sees to it that buyers and sellers are informed too—the answer is Hell, yes."

"Thank you, Mona."

"Any time."

# CHAPTER 5

## How to Go from $2,000 to $20,000 Commissions in Commercial-Industrial

> *Every person who invests in well-selected real estate in a growing section of a prosperous community adopts the surest and safest method of becoming independent, for real estate is the basis of our wealth.*
> Theodore Roosevelt

Have you found yourself irrationally resenting chocolate marshmallows on the floor of your sedan? Gum on the seat? Lip, finger, and nose droppings on the windows?

Do you erupt with hives when forced to take the nearest freeway off-ramp because Johnny Sonofaclient threw his beach ball out the window and his screams, directed into your ear, are muting the sirens of two ambulances and a fire truck?

Do you suffer morning sickness at the thought of looking another "sunny kitchen" in the face, opening the door on another "marvelous large closet"?

## Why not commercial-industrial investment?

The field offers two important advantages: (1) You will not work weekends or nights. For the woman who must contribute to the family income while keeping home, husband, and children together, this can be a crucial advantage. (But you will not lock all thoughts of business out of your mind when you lock the office doors on Friday afternoon—unless you wish to join Eloise behind the counter at Woolworth's.) (2) Commercial-industrial offers a greater profit potential than residential, considering the time expended.

"I averaged from sixty to seventy thousand dollars a year in commercial-industrial properties between 1964 and 1974," a long-time professional and one of the more successful women in the field said. "Maybe there were women in residential who did as well during that time period, but they'd have to be human dynamos, on a very demanding time schedule."

Why aren't more women in this area of real estate? Is it because most women, fearing hell-fire and damnation, hesitate to break the unwritten eleventh commandment forbidding them to engage in other than residential sales? Because most women would be ducks out of water with their powdered noses stuck in this highly competitive, business-oriented, male-dominated arena? Or is it because until very recently industrial and commercial buildings were for the most part in male brokers' hands, and they kept their fists tightly closed—or hired male police dogs, all answering to the name, "*Stayout*"?

"Not so," a male broker said emphatically, dismissing all three possibilities. "Society has brainwashed women into thinking that they're all 'home-oriented.' They're not. The sooner they realize this, the sooner you'll see them branching out into all areas of real estate."

*Preparing for a career in a different world.*

Some of the prerequisites are:

1. A genuine interest in, and an affinity for, business economics.
2. A talent for writing and research.
3. An interest in pursuing a lifetime career—rather than "dabbling in real estate because it gets me out of the house and away from the kids for a while."
4. Integrity.
5. Accuracy.
6. Patience.
7. Skill.
8. And the willingness to learn, learn, learn, learn.

Unfortunately most women engaged in residential sales do not have the education and business background necessary to go into commercial real estate. However, it is now generally agreed that a woman can be just as successful in the field as a man—if that is where her interests lie.

The key is education.

Frank Straface heads a Northern California East Bay firm (Valley Realty, affiliated with Berg Enterprises, Inc.) doing an average monthly business of $20 million.

"Suppose," I said, "that a woman came to you with no prior experience, just her license to sell real estate and the desire to start out in commercial-industrial, rather than residential. Would you hire her?"

"She'd have to come in with more than that but so would a man."

"Would you hire a woman as quickly as a man?"

"If she were qualified."

"You mean she'd have to prove herself in residential sales?"

"Not necessarily. A banking background in real estate is good experience. I've hired new licensees with that type background. Appraising is also excellent experience as a forerunner to commercial-industrial sales."

Peggy Smith, with the Washington, D.C., firm Shannon and Luchs, entered the field after eight successful years in residential real estate and graduate work in the School of Business Administration of American University. By the end of the first year in her new area, she had been involved in: a four-unit apartment, $52,000; a nineteen-unit apartment, $210,000; restaurant and apartments, $175,000; a commercial retail building, $135,000; and a townhouse-office building, $198,000; for a total of $762,000 in sales. Purchasers of investment properties buy for financial benefit. They are not swayed by emotion. For this reason, Peggy Smith said, "an agent needs to have every available fact for prospective purchasers, particularly concerning income and expense, a complete property description, copies of leases, if any, a plat, an assessment allocation for depreciation, zoning restrictions, taxes, and myriad other data. These are usually compiled in written forms and presented along with photographs and a site location map. All of this," she said, "is done prior to, and in hopes of, actually 'showing' the property."

She added a word of advice for residential agents contemplating a career in her field: "It is important to be aware of the relatively few number of openings available in most commercial departments and the huge number of requests with which most managers are swamped daily. My advice is that if you want to be a serious contender amidst all the competition, be prepared to present some substantial credentials demonstrating your willingness to devote your time and energies toward this achievement."

*Ways to break in.*

First step is, of course, to obtain a real estate license. License in hand, you should consider working for a real estate organization with residential, commercial-investment, exchange and leasing-management divisions. This will enable you to find the area you feel you could best succeed in. Your local board will in most cases have a commercial-industrial investment division chairman. Tours of properties in your area will be conducted at various times and are available free to any interested board member.

If you do not have a business background or education, are armed solely with your license to sell and a desire to enter commercial-industrial you should enroll in your local college for as many credits as you can carry in such subjects as business law, appraising, finance, economics, and taxation.

Education in these same subjects is offered by the Commercial-Industrial Investment Division of the Realtors National Marketing Institute and is available to all Realtors and Associates. The initials CCIM (Certified Commercial Investment Member) awarded by the institute upon completion of the program and after passing an examination will afford you both recognition and prestige. The education you acquire in obtaining membership will be invaluable. And as a CCIM your photo and business biography will be published annually in the institute's *Who's Who in Commercial Investment Real Estate.* You'll also have access to your fellow professionals through local chapter activities in many areas as well as through the social and educational functions at national meetings of the Marketing Institute. For information regarding content and scheduling in your area, contact Realtors National Marketing Institute, 430 North Michigan Avenue, Chicago, Illinois 60611.

Organized real estate also makes seminars and programs available to you on such subjects as commercial leasing, exchanging, real estate counseling, opportunities in urban renewal, neighborhood shopping center development, operation of a commercial-industrial real estate office, and other related aspects of the field.

Hilde Cambra was the lone woman among twelve men in a Northern California commercial-industrial firm when I interviewed her. Prior to seven years in residential sales, Hilde had a ten-year career in banking—where she was intimately involved with all phases of real estate financing as procurement officer for a bank.

"How did you break into this field?" I asked.

"I approached one of the most successful commercial-industrial firms in the area and offered them $2 million in listings if they'd take me on."

The $2 million in listings came, she explained, from builders she had worked with over a period of seven years in residential.

"Some of the men who were building residential transferred their assets and construction into commercial. I had proven myself in their residential developments and they gave me their listings."

With ten years in banking, seven years in residential, and $2 million in listings, she was taken on with the stipulation that she must sit "downstairs" with the residential people until she proved herself. Within a month she moved "upstairs."

Smartly dressed, sophisticated Charis Zeigler is owner-president of the Zeigler Company of Burbank, California. Her company is housed in attractively decorated quarters in the industrial section of the city, not far from the airport.

"Residential was not my cup of tea," she said emphatically. "I hated the night work and the weekends. There was no rapport between me and the woman looking for a home."

With a career in industrial brokerage in mind, Charis went to work for a successful industrial broker, selling homes to his clients and their employees when needed. When a vacancy occurred in the industrial sales department it was filled by a man. "And I quit," she said.

After a year as industrial director of a multi-office predominantly residential company, her former industrial broker made her an offer and she rejoined his company as an industrial salesperson. Two years later she opened her own office.

"My business is primarily industrial," she said. "It's important that women understand that commercial and industrial are dissimiliar. Our commercial work is a 'bleeding-off' from our industrial work."

"Is it more difficult to get started in this area?"

"Much more difficult. A woman should have enough money to carry her for at least a year. But the rewards are so much greater!

"Women have a lot to offer this area of the business. I'd like to see more of them in it."

Now that you have been advised of some of the necessary prerequisites for success in the field, and some of the steps taken by other women to gain entry, it would be wise for you to answer the following five questions.

1.  Do you drive the freeways, boulevards, streets and alleys calmly—no matter how many siblings may be rivaling all over your back seat?

2.  Do you experience a feeling of satisfaction upon seeing mother, father, and children settled in a home

that meets their needs—for a price they can afford to pay?

3. If you had the president of the company in your car, and were en route to two commercial investment properties, and said president mentioned that he needed a larger home for his family—would you turn around in the next driveway and take him by to see a home you felt would be "just right" for him?

4. Do you like to keep in touch with your clients after the sale to see if the children have made nice friends?

5. Somewhere between the first page of this chapter and the line before your eyes at this moment, did you thumb through the book looking for illustrations and read the last page?

If you answered "yes" to the above five questions—turn to the next chapter.

## So . . . you're going into commercial-industrial. What's it going to be like?

In an article written for *Real Estate Today* Charis Zeigler expressed her opinion of what it may be like for the woman determined to close those cupboard and closet doors forever.

"You'll make money during the first year in your new specialty but you won't make as much money as in residential sales—maybe not even enough money.

"Remember that you have a great deal to learn. Not only do you not know the answers in the beginning, you don't even understand the questions. For the first six months you may believe you will never list or sell another property. You'll be tempted to return to the world of the built-in kitchen. You must decide that your entire annual income may be sacrificed on a gamble that you will eventually earn more than you dreamed possible. You must develop an independence of attitude which includes some major changes in thinking. You are going to work from nine to five, five days a week. Your residence phone number will not appear on your cards. You will not be available most of the time except by appointment. You will have a private office.

"No more coffee with the gang, no more late nights to close with Joe, no more tours, no bullpen, no closing room, no sales contracts signed on kitchen tables, no more rain-spoiled open houses.

"And you must leave your present office. You will need an atmosphere filled with buildings and production land in order to inhale the jargon. You must get used to more zeros on the end of prices. You must learn that a good lease is no longer a second choice but often is more remunerative than a sale. Most important of all, you have to get away from houses—totally away. Decide that you will never, never list or show another home, no matter how broke you are."

## Are the years in residential sales wasted?

Opinions vary. Some women—and men—in the business feel that experience in residential is invaluable; others that the years in residential are wasted, and that residential sales people often bring bad habits into the commercial world. All agreed that it was a "different world," with different loan markets and a different type of client, needing a different sales approach, and a change in timing.

Peggy Smith feels that it is probably not a natural progression to move from residential into commercial real estate sales, but that the experience she gained in residential was extremely valuable.

"The personal contact that a successful residential

agent develops in learning to ask proper questions and actively listen to the responses are tools that will continue to be most beneficial. Successful canvassing for listings will prove useful experience, as will former practice in contract presentations. Perhaps the most valuable asset will be the manner in which time management and organization have been successfully developed."

In other areas, residential sales will not in any way prepare you for your new career and could be a minus in her opinion. You will have no preparation for the volume of correspondence confronting you, she points out, the detail work necessary for a proper cash flow analysis and internal rate of return valuation, the time-consuming preparation of formal presentations, the discouraging and financially difficult length of time which occurs between sales, and the expansive geographical territory that a commercial agent must travel.

"I've seen men," a male broker said, "come into this field with their B.A.s in Business, but with no experience in sales. And I've seen them fail and drop out. The experience gained working closely with people in the important and intimate situation of selecting a home is very beneficial."

"Should a woman gain some experience in residential sales before coming into your complex world?" I asked Charis Zeigler.

"No," she said. "Come straight in if possible. You'll learn things in residential that you'll have to unlearn here."

### Your problems in a male-dominated arena.

Once you venture into the world of shopping centers, apartment complexes, commercial blocks, and warehouses, establishing confidence in *yourself* may be your major problem.

Hang in there.

Men . . . most men no longer fear that you will break into tears if they decide not to buy your warehouse.

And when you bring in a commercial listing, your male co-workers—most male co-workers—no longer turn to one another with sly grins, to mutter behind their hands that, "Daddy must have given her the listing."

Male clients will never—well, hardly ever—step from an airplane and upon spotting you in your soft pink suit, ivory pink fingernails, and bashful blonde hair, exclaim, "My God! He's sent his secretary to meet me!"

And men no longer expect that you will flutter and coo, simply because you have eyelashes long enough to flutter and a voice capable of cooing should you so desire. (Desire should be the last thing on your mind when discussing a male client's investment dollar!)

While it is true that an occasional male client will be hard to convince that selling him an investment portfolio is not *really* what you have in mind, by and large your client will not care if you are animal, vegetable, or mineral, as long as you can make money for him—or her.

It seems appropriate to point out that a large percentage of the property in the United States is now owned by women. They, according to CII brokers and agents, are usually sharp investors. Like Virgie Turner, the black woman broker who related in an earlier chapter that she sometimes had a harder time convincing a black that she was capable of handling the sale of a home than a white, you may find it more difficult to convince a woman that you are capable of handling her investment dollar than a man.

Getting past that female secretary who insists on

knowing what you want to talk to her boss about may present more of a problem to you, as a woman. One CII broker circumvents the problem by a brief investment summary that might interest the secretary. This, she says, usually opens the mind and then the door.

Never forget, women in the business caution, that a man or woman's secretary can be very important to you. She frequently is in the driver's seat so far as time and appointments are concerned. Show respect for her position.

And *never, never*, women chorus, continue to call a prospective client back. Leave word for him to call you. Never let him think you are chasing him. By leaving a message for him to call you, maybe—just maybe—he'll get the impression that you have something he wants . . . a money-making investment.

## Federal Programs

A variety of federal programs have been enacted by Congress to entice monied investors into providing decent housing for families at rents they can afford to pay. Your investors in the 50 percent plus income tax bracket particularly benefit—recapturing their money in about five years through depreciation deductions. Set up by Congress in 1968, the National Corporation for Housing Partnerships has committed more than $51 million in equity from investors for 30,000 units with an estimated replacement cost of $575 million. HUD has put the heat on its area offices to speed up processing of applications for the program.

Under the program, families and the elderly with low and moderate incomes will pay 15 to 25 percent of their income for rent. The difference between that amount and the "market" rent for the unit will be subsidized by Uncle Sam.

Your investors typically must have a net worth in excess of $150,000 and be in the 50 percent plus income tax bracket. Normally, individual investments run more than $50,000.

The big investor in the 50 percent tax bracket can expect to get more than his original outlay back through tax deductions for accelerated depreciation in the *first four years*. It would take an investor in the 33 percent bracket eight years or longer to recapture his investment through depreciation.

In addition to the tax benefits through depreciation, your investor will obtain an annual cash flow from the project and will be building up equity.

There is no express limitation on returns because rents are geared to market levels; however, earnings on equity will usually run less than 10 percent per year.

The tax laws discourage investors from taking accelerated depreciation in the early years and then running. They must retain their interest in the project for at least ten years to obtain the benefits; otherwise excess (accelerated) depreciation is taxed as ordinary income.

## Your future in commercial-industrial investment.

If you go on to obtain your broker's license—and most women in this area of the business do—there are several options open to you.

Opening your own office makes you independent of others in your decisions, responsible only to yourself for your actions. But, you will have the twin disadvantages of high overhead and not having another broker or agent to use as a sounding board.

Even so, many women prefer to go it alone. Others find the most advantageous arrangement to be that of sharing a suite of offices with other brokers in the same field. This gives you the twin advantages of a lower overhead (since you share the services and salary of a secretary) and other brokers to bounce your ideas off.

When I asked Hilde Cambra in 1976 why she preferred operating as an independent contractor-broker with a national real estate firm to having her own firm, she replied: "Because some of the investment packages I work on run into $5 and $6 million. Getting into those figures, I feel that I must have the company name behind me (Berg Enterprises, Inc., listed on the American Stock Exchange) to gain the rapport needed with my investors."

In 1978, Hilde established her own firm, Cambra and Associates, in Oakland, California.

Hilde's fee as a contract negotiator is $50.00 an hour. Her background? She married at fifteen and went back to school for a high school diploma after she had two babies. "And, I've been studying ever since, finance, appraising, taxation. For the past year or so I've concentrated on real estate law. I plan to take California's mini-bar this year."

Membership in SIR (Society of Industrial Realtors), a prestigious international organization, is a possibility in your future. The stated objectives of SIR are: "To unite those Realtors engaged in buying, selling, or leasing land and buildings to industry; the fostering of knowledge, education, integrity and quality workmanship in the field of industrial real estate; the exchange of information among members; mutual cooperation in exchange of listings and sound services to owners and users of industrial real estate; certification, identification, and qualification of experienced and competent industrial property brokers; and cooperation with all governmental and civic organizations, public utilities, and financial institutions."

For information on basic membership qualifications, contact Society of Industrial Realtors, 925 15th Street, N.W., Washington, D.C., 20005—or your local board.

One of the most exciting occurrences in the field is the availability of a centralized computer for listing commercial or industrial properties, providing exposure to prospective buyers throughout the country. This computerized data bank also lists the needs of those in the market to buy. The information is available via a computer printout to subscribers. The printouts list properties by state and region within states, rather than nationally, to hold membership costs to a minimum. Data are provided as to location, type of property, land and building size. Only information authorized by the broker or owner is listed.

The service does not constitute competition for brokers or anyone else. It is strictly a listing service. A membership fee is charged subscribers but there is no involvement with commission arrangements, the price being asked, terms of sale, etc. The service is available to any board member upon request, and there are no territorial limitations.

### Real estate's billion-dollar party. Will you be invited?

The first billion-dollar real estate party was held in Houston in November 1976. Tickets to the party cost $175, but the key to the invitation list was what each guest brought—properties with a minimum price tag of $1 million.

The invitees were the "who's who" of the national financial and real estate institutions—principals who buy or sell for their own account such as pension funds, insurance companies, banks, developers, and a variety of foreign investment groups; and brokers who have exclusive or written authorization to represent principals in like properties.

The event was called AMREX Market Day and was sponsored by AMREX (American Real Estate Exchange) a data communications company operating securities information systems nationwide, and First American Title Insurance Company.

"Unlike stock and bond markets," said Gerald Jackson, president of AMREX, "which are auction markets, large-scale real estate is bought and sold in a negotiated market. Thus, the advantage of attending market day is primarily to participate in the acceleration of finding good properties and buyers, and initiating transactions. Also, the personal, informal contacts made at this event lead to lasting business relationships."

Market Day procedures are relatively simple. Attendees preregister and presubmit their properties and buying constraints on a confidential form weeks in advance of Market Day. When they enter the "trading floor" they are handed a confidential binder containing the entire inventory of the day's event. Each property and buyer's demands are described in brief form and categorized for quick reference.

A buyer or seller wishing to pursue a particular situation jots down on a paging slip his or her trading number and also the number assigned to that property in the binder. The slip is handed to the paging platform, and the counterpart is paged. The parties are formally introduced and may retire to a staging area to discuss a potential transaction in private.

Participants are exposed to three to four hundred situations at Market Day. The system allows each to sort those situations that fit his or her needs. By the time the late afternoon cocktail party begins, attendees may have met and personally discussed forty to fifty situations, established ten to twenty key business relationships, and have in his or her briefcase five to ten possible transactions. What normally would take weeks and months of searching and traveling nationally has been compressed into one day.

AMREX expects to have trading floors in Los Angeles, San Francisco, New York, Boston, Chicago, Atlanta, Houston, and Dallas—all lined together electronically.

Will you one day be on the guest list of real estate's billion-dollar party?

## Summing it up.

Yes, Virginia, you *can* get out of the linen closet, and into the warehouse. Training is available. There is no age barrier. And, there is no masculine mystique. There is really only one basic requirement. *Prepare yourself!* If that cash flow analysis and internal rate of return valuation are put together shoddily with inadequate knowledge and inferior attention, and that industrial complex roof comes crashing down on your hairdo, you're going to be a lot more conspicuous standing amid the rubble in high heels, manicured nails, and clinging jersey dress than would your male counterpart.

# CHAPTER 6

# How to Get Out of the House and onto the Land

*So simple is the earth we tread,*
*So quick with love and life her frame;*
*Ten thousand years have dawned and fled,*
*And still her magic is the same.*
Stopford A. Brooke
*"The Earth and Man"*

Two words in the Hawaiian language mean land. The first *honua*, is sometimes translated as earth. The second, *aina*, refers to land as a place of attachment—of special significance to a person.

Slim, fashionable Raechel Parker, headquartered in a Waikiki Beach high-rise, offers "some of the most beautiful land left on this earth."

She may show a cattle ranch at Kipahulu on Maui for $2,500,000; two-thousand acres with three miles of ocean front on the island of Hawaii for $22,500,000; an organic farm at Pupukea, Oahu, for $160,000; a small cottage set on white sand with a swimming beach at Kailua Bay for $345,000.

She will fly you to the Fiji Islands for a look at hardwood timber property with no taxes, on the Ndreketi River; or to Rarotonga Titikaveka in the Cook Islands to consider a studio cottage with lagoon frontage.

Once upon a time (look over your shoulder and you're there) such words and phrases as square, tract, section, acre, metes and bounds, base and meridian lines were considered part of a supermale language, a language that females were incapable of speaking, writing, or reading—much less selling! The mental picture of a woman with her heels mired in the mud of the diagrammed section below, curls and skirt blowing in the wind, and a puzzled look on her powdered features would have brought howls of merriment and stares of disbelief from most males in the real estate profession.

1 mile

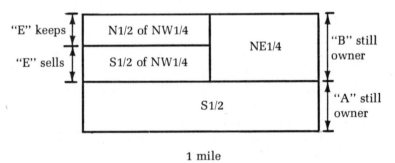

1 mile

How could a member of a sex capable of losing herself, her children, her dog, and the family station wagon between her place of residence and the supermarket, one-half mile and six corners away, be expected to "begin at a point located at the NW corner of the SW1/2 of the NW1/2 of Section 12; thence south 3/4 of a mile, thence east 1/2 mile, thence in a straight line back to the point of the beginning"—without losing her buyer in the south forty and filling the well bucket with frustrated tears?

It stood to reason that if females were incapable of learning the male-oriented land language, their more delicately formed fingers were incapable of picking up the 10 (sometimes 17 to 18) percent commissions customarily paid on unimproved land.

In spite of the fact that it is sometimes harder for a woman to overcome her own self-doubts than those of buyers, sellers, and male professionals, female names are now to be found on contracts written on farms and unimproved land in every state in the nation.

Mary Howe is developing and packaging highway property for commercial and industrial use in Largo, Florida. Edna Martin, of El Centro, California, is leasing, selling, exchanging, appraising, and managing farm property. Mary Manderson is in farm and land in Alabama, Laurie Jablin in Georgia, Nellie Robbins in Indiana and Robi Francisco in California. Annette Jones is selling, appraising, and exchanging recreational, farm, and commercial-industrial land in Virginia.

The fabulously successful Dixie Williams of Miami Shores, Florida, has sold farm, sugar cane, or grazing pasture land to clients from Guatemala, Colombia, Peru, Brazil, and Argentina. The night I interviewed her, she had flown Spanish investors to Kentucky and West Virginia to look at coal reserves. Most of her land offerings are shown by helicopter.

Among her recent sales was one for between thirty and forty thousand acres of Florida farm land to a conglomerate for a price in excess of $1,000,000. "An old Florida Cracker listed it with me," she said. "He's the biggest individual owner left in the State of Florida. I took it on a 5 percent commission. I never argue commissions."

In 1966, the 5'2" auburn-haired, green-eyed Miss Williams bought a large tract of land in Miami and began a three-year rezoning battle with the city fathers. To aid her, she hired a research economist and Hank Meyers, one of the best known public relations men in the country. Five years later, on December 30, 1971, she sold the last parcel of the original purchase, receiving more than $1 million profit—all expenses (including that of Mr. Meyers' services) deducted.

Seventy-six one-acre lots in the development were set aside for residential purposes. "I sold them to a contractor for $125,000 in 1971. In 1976, he listed the seventy-six with me at $200,000. He was willing to pay the full 10 percent commission of $20,000 when I brought in a buyer."

Another recent sale involved 158.5 acres of Florida land for $750,000 for an apartment complex.

With Florida pasture land running from $500 to $3,250 an acre, row crop land $750 or $850 an acre, sugar cane land in the Lake Okeechobee area $3,500 to $4,500 an acre (must be recognized by a sugar cane mill to be valuable) and selling in parcels of 100 to 50,000 acres, it is understandable that the ladylike Dixie does not argue commissions with her clients. And she believes in her product. She owns 3,400 acres in cattle land and 180 acres in tomatoes. She is also part owner of a coal mining company in Kentucky.

Blonde Mary Lou Melville, one of two accredited farm and land brokers in Montana (the other is a man), frankly admits that most of her transactions are for a million dollars or more.

"Most of the large ranches are sold in sections rather than acres. A section is 640 acres, and it's not uncommon to handle 80 section ranches."

Before her marriage to a Montana rancher, Mary Lou

owned a multiple office in California with fifty-two salespeople working for her. Now her only employee is a secretary, "because I'm on the go so much of the time." A member of the worldwide Society of Exchange Counselors, she has transactions that may involve the exchange of a $2 million Montana ranch for commercial property in France or West Germany or a medical building in New York City for 50,000 acres in Canada.

"Ranchers don't buy the big holdings now. They're bought by conglomerates or other large investors."

Obviously it is possible for women to learn that a section is not just something the beauty parlor parts your hair into when giving you a permanent; ranch is not the plural of range; tract is not the root of subtract; and a square can have a meaning other than that which you divide the brownies into before the kids come home from school.

## How to open the door and get out of the house.

Like commercial-industrial, farm and land is a highly specialized area of real estate, requiring education, expertise, and experience. For most women the first step toward success in farm and land has been membership in the Farm and Land Institute. Organized in 1944, the Institute is devoted exclusively to brokers and agents involved in various phases of land development and land utilization. The privilege of joining the institute and taking advantage of its educational programs is afforded all members of the National Association of Realtors.

"Let's face it," said one successful woman broker—in real estate for thirty years and in farm and land exclusively for the last twenty—"women come into real estate knowing how many cupboards a kitchen has to have in order to store a respectable number of pots, pans, dishes, and staples. They know that a house should have a linen closet—unless they're showing it to an idiot. They know a hell of a lot about houses—more than most men. That's why they do so well. But, about farm and land? What do they know? The smattering of information they pick up in the process of getting a license is probably forgotten by the time they're notified that they passed the state exam.

"What does the average woman who gets her real estate license think a 'package' is?" she asked.

"Something she picks up at the supermarket, or something the mailman delivers," she answered.

"No woman," she said emphatically, "should attempt to sell farm and land until she's qualified to do so. The uneducated woman attempting to sell in this area is an embarrassment to knowledgeable women, and to the entire industry."

California Realtor Robi Francisco, designated an Accredited Farm and Land Broker by the Farm and Land Institute, underscored that anonymous opinion with, "In this business we should be informed under all circumstances, but it's imperative in this particular area of our business.

"Sometimes," she explained, "we have clients acquiring tracts of land, or putting together small tracts with the intention of holding them for a period to determine high and best use. The properties may be marketed as a total package to a developer or divided into smaller packages and sold to individual developers. It's imperative that we consult lawyers, appraisers, etc."

The Farm and Land Institute brings together brokers and agents interested in selling, exchanging, managing, appraising, financing, or developing land; fosters and establishes educational activities; and identifies to the public those brokers and agents who are members and, therefore, subject to the standards and discipline of the institute.

Active members consist of farm and land brokers elected by the Board of Governors of the institute. Associate membership is open to agents associated with Realtors (and holding membership in a local board of the National Association). The prestigious designation AFLB (Accredited Farm and Land Broker) requires additional education and experience. To achieve the status, FLI members must have fulfilled requirements prescribed by the Designations Committee and approved by the Board of Governors for both candidacy and designation.

Regular services for members include: a monthly news bulletin, *The Farm and Land Realtor*, containing articles by recognized authorities on topics pertaining to land, exchange of business-building ideas and practices between members, factual data as the result of surveys and committee reports; a roster of members issued annually to enable direct contact; a farm and land brokers' manual containing information and statistical data for everyday use; the highly successful marketing sessions; and educational courses to keep members current on all phases of land development.

Jeanne Oare, of Pompano Beach, Florida, cited a recent three-way exchange involving an Iowa farm, a Chicago apartment property, and a Florida planned unit development as an example of the benefits afforded by membership in the institute. "Such an exchange, involving properties in three different states, would not have been possible without a national organization," she said. (Jeanne is owner-operator of a firm dealing almost entirely in farm and land. The seven agents associated with her firm are all men.)

Educational activities include one- to four-day seminars throughout the year in various locations, covering such subjects as property rights, land use, ground leasing, urban land brokerage, agricultural land brokerage, taxation, financing, discounted cash flow analysis, internal rate of return—and a host of related subjects.

The highly acclaimed four-and-one-half- and three-and-one-half-day courses "Agricultural and Urban Land Brokerage" and "Land Return Analysis" are presented several times each year in various strategically located cities. The authoritative text on taxation, *Federal Taxes Affecting Real Estate*, is distributed within the National Association exclusively by the Farm and Land Institute, and is updated by special supplements issued as new tax laws are analyzed.

## The farm as an investment.

Should you advise buyers looking for a place to put their investment dollars to consider a farm? "Yes," said attractive Marie Sullivan, and pointed to the fact that international investors are buying up American agricultural land at an unprecedented pace. "Perhaps they feel that food-producing land will be the last great investment."

The godchild of Abel Pierce Borden, of Borden milk fame (responsible for bringing the first Brahman cattle from India to this country), Marie sells farm and land in four counties in the Houston, Texas, area. Her properties range from 50 acres to 4,000 acres, with an average price of $1,200 an acre. She obtained an agent's license in 1969, a broker's license in 1971, "because you need the added knowledge," and her first farm listing in 1971—at 5:30 A.M.

"If you can be here at 5:30 tomorrow morning,"

rancher John Martin told her, "I'll give you the listing on my property."

"Here" was seventy miles from Marie's home, but she got the listing—750 acres of grazing land at $750.00 an acre—a $562,500 prize.

Your farm investor, Marie explained, can either pay cash, accept a modest annual return and wait for growth over a fairly long period, or invest a minimum of cash and look for maximum leverage on the cash investment. Farmland is a prime candidate for leverage, since so much of it is financed by the seller. Private contracts can be made with as little as 10 percent down, and conventional financing over twenty to thirty years is available, but usually requires a down payment of one-third to one-half of the purchase price.

Contract selling can spread the taxes due when the investor sells. By selling for a small down payment and carrying the contract over a ten or fifteen-year period, capital gains tax can be spread over the life of the contract.

Your investor may rent his farm at an agreed upon amount per acre for row crop land, or per head (for grazing land), and pay taxes, insurance, and maintenance. The tenant farmer provides the equipment, labor, and knowledge and keeps anything he earns above the rent, giving the tenant the opportunity to amortize his investment in equipment, without tying up capital in land.

Some investors prefer hiring someone to run the farm for wages. The investor provides equipment and seed, pays for upkeep, and assumes all risks. He also keeps all the profits—if any. The obvious drawback to this plan is that the employee lacks any incentive to show profit.

Investors can also be advised to consider the share-lease arrangement—investor provides the land and certain costs of production, and the tenant supplies the labor and know-how and shares the production costs. The risk and profit are then split—usually fifty-fifty.

If your investor is interested in hiring a professional farm manager to oversee his investment, women in farm and land repeatedly say, "Contact the American Society of Farm Managers and Rural Appraisers in Denver, Colorado." For a fee ranging from 6 to 10 percent of the owner's gross, a professional farm manager will locate a tenant, prepare a budget, provide monthly income-expense statements, and work out a cropping system. He will also arrange insurance coverage, pay taxes, invest funds until they're needed for seeds or fertilizer, and arrange maintenance. Fees vary with the service expected of the manager, but the investor should expect this method to take .5 percent or so off his net income.

## The owner-operated small farm.

Many urban and suburban families are now seeking a different way of life—sometimes giving up the security of a high salary to relocate their families in a rural atmosphere. The rural housing division of the Farmers Home Administration reports an accelerated rate of inquiries and applications being received. Farm and land sales are up in most states and the trend is expected to continue. In some areas activity in the residential field does not match that in the farm and land market.

Most sales of small farms are financed by the seller. But if seller-financing is not available, and your buyer cannot qualify for conventional financing, the Farm Home Mortgage program under the Department of Agriculture may be a financial source.

Loans are made in rural areas classified as open country and towns with a population of 10,000 or less (under some circumstances, in towns with populations between 10,000 and 20,000 outside of standard metropolitan statistical areas). Homes may be built on individual tracts or in subdivisions, and your buyers may purchase an existing house and lot, or a site on which to build.

Loans for the development of rental housing in rural areas are also available through FMHA for certain investor clients.

Your modest or low-income buyer should be advised to investigate farm operating loans (accompanied by technical management assistance), farm emergency loans, irrigation and drainage loans, grazing association loans, soil and water conservation loans, and recreation enterprise loans (for individual farms planning income-producing outdoor on-farm recreation).

## The case for unimproved land.

There is a growing tendency among Americans to invest in land rather than the stock market according to a survey conducted by Investors Mortgage Insurance Company of Boston.

"Vacant land," said Frank Kinst, president of an Illinois savings and loan association, "shows the greatest appreciation without worry about rents and maintenance. Land that is built upon doesn't realize the same rise in value as well-selected unimproved property."

Questioned about the wisdom of holding land for years with ever increasing taxes and interest rates, he replied: "Maybe it will cost as much as 10 percent of the purchase price each year to hold, but for a $2,000 piece of land to appreciate to $10,000 has been common in our experience." Investors, he pointed out, could not get that kind of return any other way. But investors should be advised to forget the cash they are putting into the land and plan to keep it for ten or fifteen years, said Frank Kinst. "They aren't paying off a loan, they're making an investment."

As in residential and commercial-industrial sales, it is difficult to find a woman knowledgeable in farm and land who is not investing in her product. Some women, by practicing what they preach, have built substantial estates investing in unimproved land. They point to the fact that land values have doubled in the last five years. In thirteen states, they doubled in four years or less. Perhaps Scottsdale, Arizona, provides the most spectacular example—land in some areas went from $5 an acre to $8,500 an acre in fifteen years!

The accelerated use of land for recreation, airports, schools, subdivisions, etc., makes for keen competition for prime acreage and creates undreamed of opportunities for farm and land professionals. Example: A new town, The Woodlands, is being built on 20,000 acres of Texas land—three schools, an industrial park, shopping centers, conference center, country club and golf course, swim and athletic center, and 47,000 dwelling units!

Some women have assured their financial future simply by investing in the right vacant lot at the right time. The success story of residential building lots in certain California communities makes real estate professionals who passed them up as "overpriced" in the sixties contemplate reaching for the overdose bottle.

You can, according to a Sunday ad in the *Los Angeles Times: "BUILD YOUR DREAM HOME RIGHT ABOVE DANA HARBOR, 9500 SQ FT R-1 LOTS . . . $148,500."*

Two lots recently went on the market on Carmel's seventeen-mile drive—one-and-one-half acres for $150,000, and one-and-one-fourth acres for $125,000.

In 1960, residential lots could be bought in the Palos Verdes Estates area for $10,000. Today, lots without an ocean view bring $60,000 and up; with a view, $100,000 and up—depending on the amount of sea you wish to observe from your bedroom window.

"Use your license to invest," said Vera Rivers of San Rafael, California. "Don't wait for that better day, or better buy. Buy whatever you can afford at the time."

In 1938, Vera bought the home she now occupies for $1,950—$300 down, and $25 a month. In the forties she bought the adjoining vacant lot for $500, and put in a swimming pool. In 1976, she turned down an offer of $100,000 for her property.

In 1949, when Ruth Johnston was with the Harry H. Kam Company (one of the original subdividers of Beverly Hills), Mrs. Cooley Butler gave her a plot of the land that today comprises Truesdale Estates in Bel Air and asked her to find a buyer. "Had I been able to sell the idea of subdividing it to a developer in 1949, the lots would probably have sold for around $3,000 or $4,000. When the property was finally bought and subdivided in the fifties, the lots sold for $40,000 to $50,000. Now? Who knows? $100,000 and up, if there were any left."

"In the early fifties," she reminisced, "we used to drive by the old Cotton estate in San Clemente, on our way to a beach-town Mexican restaurant. The place had been vacant about fifteen years at that time, and we used to wonder what would happen to it."

"What did?"

"A man named Nixon bought it."

## Income opportunities in recreational land.

Dreams of owning a lodge in the mountains, a cabin by the shore, vacant property in a recreational area, are becoming realities for more and more Americans—creating unprecedented opportunities for land specialists.

In four years, it is estimated by Investors Mortgage Insurance Company of Boston, more than ten million American families will own two homes or a home and a second lot. And contrary to popular belief, owning recreational property is no longer a luxury limited to the rich. IMIC's survey found that two-thirds of the two-home families earn from $16,000 to $25,000 a year and that nearly three-fourths earn less than $44,000 annually. The majority of existing second homes are located in the Northeast, the Midwest, and Florida; the largest share of the country's subdivided but undeveloped properties are in the Sun Belt states of Florida, Texas, New Mexico, Arizona, and California. Whether you hang your license north, south, east or west, you can participate in the recreational land trend.

Traditionally, spaces in mobile home parks have been rented; however, new laws now allow real estate licensees to sell both mobile homes and own-your-own lots in most states. The sale of these homes combined with the sale of the lot offers a double opportunity for income. In one California county doing a brisk business in own-your-own mobile home lots, ten parks showed a total of 3,841 spaces ranging in size from 5,000 to 72,000 square feet—for as low as $6,450, and as high as $24,950. Some parks are identical in appearance to regular middle-class housing tracts except for the dwelling unit. Others offer golf courses, swimming pools, saunas, recreation rooms, etc. In one of the larger, country-club-type developments, 1,081 mobile home lots sell for $10,950 to $24,950; and when the lots and mobile homes are sold together, prices soar as high as $150,000!

I found Lucille Cummins dressed in orange slacks and brown boots selling quarter- to half-acre ponderosa pine-covered California mountain lots. "They can be used for mobile or conventional homes," she said.

The development boasted such attractions as fishing, water skiing, boating, tennis courts, golf course, equestrian center and riding trails, pool, clubhouse, and a modern shopping center.

The entire sales force—half of them women—lived in the development, she explained.

"What commission do you work on?"

"Seven percent. We used to get 17 or 18 percent when we opened up, but we're pretty well sold out now, so we're down to 7."

"What about the fact that mobile homes depreciate in value—how do you counter that objection?"

"They don't. Not if they're placed in a well-maintained development. They appreciate—as the lot itself appreciates in value."

The green trees, orange slacks, and peaceful pine-scented air seemed part of a farm and land world far removed from sleek international exchanges of forty-section ranches for European shopping centers, Argentinian holdings for New York medical centers. "I suppose the women don't expect to make more than pin money here," I offered.

"Thirty thousand is a pretty good year for me," she said icily.

The popularity of campers, tent trailers, and camping out in general has resulted in still another opportunity for the land professional—own-your-own campsites.

Such developments have various amenities—swimming pools, hobby centers, and game and sporting activities. They are much like rental campgrounds, except that they are owned by the campers, with the owners paying a monthly maintenance charge.

It is imperative, say knowledgeable women, that the real estate professional planning to develop land for recreational use, or counseling a buyer in such an area, turn to the land planners for guidance. Land planners have engineering departments schooled in market studies. They are able to plan budgets and watch the cash flow, and they know the cost factors involved.

Personnel selected to sell a recreational development must be fully informed as to the use to which the land can be put, and must know the tax structure; no easy task, women agree, because there can be constant changes in regulations, generated by county, state, and sometimes HUD.

Is the recreational land boom a flash in the real estate pan? A here-this-year—gone-next-year source of income for land specialists? Not according to Jackson Goss, president of Investors Mortgage Insurance Company.

"Recent surveys," concludes Mr. Goss, "indicate that the second home and recreational land markets will continue to grow—as will their potential for creating positive environmental, economic, and social impacts throughout this decade and into the 1980s."

## Taking your product to market.

One of the services the Farm and Land Institute provides its members is the opportunity to participate in marketing sessions, both national and regional. National sessions are held in conjunction with each national meeting, while the regional sessions are held in various parts of the country throughout the year.

Millions of dollars in property are offered for sale, lease, or exchange at these sessions, with highly qualified moderators guiding the presentations. With the moderator's aid and the cooperation of other participants, your listings will be exposed in a manner calculated to bring about their successful marketing. Be sure that you come to market well prepared. Have sufficient printouts of back-up information on your properties to pass out to each attendee.

Robert W. Van Arsdale, a past president of the Farm and Land Institute, has this to say about marketing sessions (excerpted from *The Farm and Land Realtor*):

"These are the 'nuts and bolts' sessions, which reach your pocketbook with fees. If you are not participating in marketing sessions, you are missing the opportunity to be of service to your clients by successfully marketing their properties—and to yourself by making money.

"The neophyte or uninformed might say, 'No one in New Mexico (California, Illinois, New Jersey, Florida or whatever) wants the property I have to offer.' However, investors are buying properties in all parts of the country and world. We never know where that customer or investor may be. We can no longer look to our local area or to geographical limits and be successful in marketing properties. Investors no longer have hang-ups about crossing state lines, and are very prone to go to the areas they may feel offer particular advantages in rounding out their real property portfolios.

"It is necessary that we explore all possibilities. Investors are moving their interests all over these United States—and foreign countries.

"Transportation has now opened the world to the real estate professional. Companies are seeking suitable locations for overseas plants and offices; hotel chains and airlines are planning resort and vacation facilities in newly accessible areas; emerging nations are potential sources for valuable investment and development programs. Conversely, foreign interests are buying more and more American property and looking for additional ways to invest in the United States."

## Avoiding the pitfalls.

Will you go to market with a truckload of choice listings, or a basket of culls? Will your farm listings consist of lush, fertile bottomland, or rocky hillside plots where your potential buyer risks falling to the highway below?

As in commercial-industrial, the key to success for women in farm and land is—*education!* The successful farm and land professional must be able to evaluate land-use trends, and read land-price movements indicating profit potential for investors. She must know how to judge a property's utility and financial capability so that her clients know how much land to buy or sell at any one time for the greatest return on investment. She knows the specialized lending sources available for her investor. The sources for undeveloped land loans. The best interim income-producing use for a particular property. How to finance the purchase of transitional land.

"How does the farm and land area of real estate differ from residential?" I asked California FLI member Jane Fairchild.

"Basically, it doesn't differ from any other area," she said, "because all successful firms become so through referrals from satisfied clients.

"Just as the successful residential professional does not 'palm-off' a poor house on an unsuspecting buyer, so it is with the successful woman in this area. Not every piece of land is a good investment. Water must be available, the soil must be good, weather is important, of course, and the stability of the land.

"But it does differ in that a house is for living, while land can be put to many uses. Determining the highest and best use for a property calls for both knowledge and imagination. In this sense, selling land is like selling ideas."

Robi Francisco of Sun City, California, has been in real estate for twenty-three years, a broker for twenty-one years. In addition to membership in the Farm and Land Institute, she is a member of the International Real Estate Federation and of the International Council of Industrial Developers.

"Are there mistakes made that apply particularly to farm and land?" I asked her.

"Yes. Failure to get an exclusive listing is always a mistake. There are so many legalities, so many details to see to—zoning, land use—and special requirements here where we must worry about earthquakes. In the Midwest and South brokers must worry about cyclonic paths. And we have to work with the county, the state, and sometimes HUD. So much of your time is involved; you must have control of the property."

A second mistake to avoid at all costs, Robi said, is that of not listing the property long enough. "Larger properties take longer to sell, especially the border-type properties not particularly good for agriculture and without much possibility of urban development.

"In most farm or ranch areas there are three selling seasons in a year. From January until April there is the serious farmer or rancher who wants to buy early enough to get his crop in, then from about June until September you'll get the investors looking. Late in the year you'll get prospects who've had a high-income year and want to find an investment before the end of the tax year. In this area of Southern California, our buying season is determined largely by the weather, the heat, and the rain.

"Explain these things to your clients," she emphasized. "Listings on farm and land should be for one year and should be exclusive."

Inquiries from overseas brokers and buyers have accelerated in the past few years, Robi said. "Most of my clients are from Canada and South America. Sometimes they phone from their country. Sometimes they just drop in."

"Farm and land is not for every woman," Marie Sullivan of Houston warned. "You have to be prepared for most anything.

"Most anything," she explained, could be watching a lady prospect throw off all her clothes and jump into a nearby stream when thousands of chiggers swarmed out of a bush and over her body.

"Be prepared to return from five-mile hikes with blistered feet," said Marie. "Always wear long sleeve shirts and pants. Keep your boots in the car. And don't forget to carry insecticide."

First presentations should be made from the office with the use of pictures, Marie said. "Prospective buyers must take time off from busy schedules to view properties. Don't waste their time, and yours, by showing properties that do not meet their needs or tastes.

"And be sure that you have all the information on a property before taking a prospect out. If you're pleased with yourself because you know how high that hill is to the right of the house, they're going to wipe the smile off your face with: 'How deep is the well?' And if you know what kind of timber is on the back lot, chances are they won't mention timber. They'll want to know what that grain is on the front acreage.

"And particular consideration must be shown your farm sellers. There's a saying that the difference between a cattleman and a farmer is that a cattleman can sell anything and never look back, but when a farmer sells his farm, it's like taking out a piece of his heart."

A fine arts major in college, Marie switched from residential sales to farm and land because: "Some of the homes I showed were built with such poor taste that I couldn't in good conscience become enthusiastic.

"But I can become euphoric over a tract of land. No one has been there to spoil the beauty."

Of the 5,200 members of the Farm and Land Institute, approximately 5 percent are women. Of the 350 Accredited Farm and Land Brokers, 22 are women. Admittedly, farm and land is still largely a man's world, but every year a few more women close the "extra large closet" door, open the kitchen screen door—and step out onto the land.

"Why are more and more women becoming successful in this male-dominated area of the business?" I asked a male broker.

"For the same reasons they're successful in residential sales. They're willing to learn. They work hard. They're patient.

"Sometimes," he said, "I think they care a little more."

# CHAPTER 7

## Taking Advantage of Investment Opportunities

*Ninety percent of all millionaires became so through owning real estate. More money has been made in real estate than in all industrial investments combined.*
Andrew Carnegie

*Foiling the greatest bank robber in history.*

The best investment in the world is United States real estate.

Enough foreign investors believe this to be true to have given two investment counseling companies—one from England and one from Canada—a $250 million checkbook to buy American property. The total amount of funds is unlimited according to representatives of the foreign investment partnership of Donald H. Bodel, senior vice-president of A. E. LePage of Canada, and Christopher D. Budden, senior vice-president of Richard Ellis of London.

"We're here as agents for foreign investors," Donald Bodel said at the opening of the company's U.S. headquarters in Chicago.

Christopher Budden, a London native, believes that this country is where the United Kingdom was twenty years ago. "At that time, government controls limited new construction so much that people who owned real estate realized enormous appreciation. That is now happening here."

He pointed out that in areas of this country where there is very little construction, critical shortages will soon develop. "Then there will be a rapid escalation of rents, and properties will become much more valuable."

Knowledgeable women agreed with Christopher Budden's appraisal of American property long before he, and other foreign investors, discovered America. It would be difficult to find a woman with an active real estate license who is not investing in the commodity she sells. Some use their licenses solely for their own investments.

"Some of the largest percentage profits today are being made by women who started out with from $1,000 to $10,000 nest eggs," broker Claire Lowther of Kaneohe, Hawaii, said. "In most cases the nest egg was saved from commissions earned in this business.

"I've watched residential land climb to around $3.00 a square foot in the Honolulu area. I sold a house for $69,000 in 1972. The identical house sold for $110,000 in 1975. Two bedroom condominiums in a building on Ward Street could be bought for $45,000 to $48,000 in 1968. Today you couldn't touch one for less than $150,000."

The secret of successful investing, Claire said, is not waiting until you can afford a warehouse or a complex. "Pick up any good buy that comes along, a single-family dwelling, a duplex—whatever you can afford, no matter how small."

Our savings in most institutions are insured against

theft by robbers who carry guns, but not against the greatest of all thieves—inflation. Each time there is a fractional increase in the cost of living, there is a corresponding fractional decrease in the purchasing power of our money. The dollar amount in our bank books may remain the same, but in terms of what those dollars will buy, the robbery has been just as real as if a masked bandit had held us up on the street and taken a portion of our hard-earned savings. If government figures reveal that a mere three-tenths of one percent cost of living has taken place, and another news item reveals that total savings are $350 billion—inflation has entered the vaults of American banks and stolen over a billion dollars. It happens almost every month! And women in the business are convinced that real estate offers the best hedge against inflation—the greatest bank robber in history.

Northern California broker Maryanne Ingemanson, in the business since 1960, is principal owner of more than a half-dozen major commercial properties in her area of the state. These include a 142-space mobile home park, a large warehouse, two downtown office buildings (rented to state and municipal agencies), and a prime office building in a blue chip suburban area, among others.

Ingemanson Enterprises has developed and sold a sixty-four-unit apartment house and a two-story dental office building. The firm owns other property ranging from a modern service station unit to a well-designed suburban dental office.

Three years after Maryanne became a self-employed broker, she was averaging more than $3 million annually in business property sales. It was at this time that she began to develop improved properties in the name of Ingemanson Enterprises.

"My ideas had worked for other people, so I decided to apply them to my own firm. I built an 89,000 square-foot warehouse on five and one-half acres in Sacramento's port area, and leased it to the California Division of State Records."

Her second project was a new five-star mobile home park (which Ingemanson Enterprises has retained); the next project, a sixty-eight-unit apartment complex, sold after completion.

Maryanne handles all the details of her own developments and those of her group of thirty or so regular investment customers who live all over California and as far east as Iowa and Illinois.

"I keep the records and tell the accountants the information they need for income tax records. I love math, the kind of science that proves itself out. That's probably one reason I was drawn to real estate."

What is Maryanne's background? A Certified Public Accountant, perhaps? A university business graduate? A former math teacher? A licensed building contactor?

Well . . . no. At fifteen she performed Tschaikovsky's Piano Concerto with the San Francisco Symphony Orchestra under the direction of Leopold Stokowski and thereafter traveled throughout the world presenting solo recitals or performing with symphonic groups in Germany, Amsterdam, and the prestigious Albert Hall in London. At twenty-two she married, and at twenty-six she turned to real estate.

### *The four variable factors of investment— and their relation to real estate.*

Financial analyst Robert Bruss, a California attorney, licensed broker and syndicated columnist, names the four variable factors of any investment in the United States: (1) safety; (2) market value appreciation; (3) yield; and (4) liquidity, and relates them to real estate.

Concerning the first factor, "safety," he finds that: "Real estate holds its value and increases in value far better than other investment alternatives, and with less downside risk." As proof of this he points out that mortgage lenders will loan a higher percentage of value in real estate than on any other type of investment security, and for a longer term—often up to thirty years or more.

Discussing the second factor, "market value appreciation," he points out that: "real property has two major factors that tend to force its value constantly higher: (1) increasing demand from an increasing population for a limited supply of well-located land, and (2) inflationary cost increases of new construction which make existing properties more valuable than their original construction cost." He stresses the importance of location as the key to appreciation and the need to check market trends.

Analyzing the third factor, "yield," he finds that real estate investments far surpass any other type of equity for consistent yield and cites two major reasons: "(1) property yields appreciation in market value of 5 percent to 10 percent per year, or more, to keep pace with or surpass the inflation rate, and (2) the tax advantages of owning property, especially depreciable property, further enhance the yield an additional 3 percent to 20 percent or more per year, depending upon the investor's tax bracket. Yields of 10 percent to 30 percent total, or more, are not uncommon in real estate investments."

And, discussing the fourth factor, "liquidity," he notes that many novice investors are under the false impression that real estate lacks liquidity. "While it certainly isn't as liquid as a savings account, most real estate can be sold within thirty days for its fair market value." Property on the market for a longer period is, he believes, due to unrealistic pricing by sellers.

## Real estate's twin advantages.

### 1. LEVERAGE.

"Leverage" means investing the least amount of capital possible when acquiring a property in order to earn the maximum percentage return on the investment. For example, Agent Mary Smith and Agent Jane Jones own identical buildings worth $100,000 each. Mary owns her building free and clear while Jane has an $80,000 mortgage.

If the value of each building goes up 10 percent, Mary has increased her equity by 10 percent, from $100,000 to $110,000. But Jane's equity has soared up 50 percent from $20,000 to $30,000. If Mary had bought five mortgaged buildings instead of one free and clear, her rise in equity would have been five times as great with the same initial investment.

Stan Herman, one of Beverly Hill's most successful brokers relates a story to illustrate leverage.

Mary Douvan, one of his top agents, was driving oil-rich Iranian clients to Santa Barbara to buy a shopping center. She mentioned that the Harold Lloyd estate was going up for auction the next day.

"What'll it sell for?" asked one of her passengers.

"Probably a million and a half," Mary told him.

A mile or two ticked by, then from the back seat, one of her passengers said: "OK, let's buy it."

At 4 P.M. that day Stan Herman was showing the mansion to them. By 10 A.M. the following day, the Iranians were back in his house, shedding diamonds and travelers' checks trying to come up with $250,000 to qualify for the bidding. They had come prepared to buy a shopping center with a check, not an estate with cash.

The crisis was averted when Mr. Herman persuaded the auctioneers that his friends were "solid." They bid on trust, and purchased the property for $1.6 million, putting down $700,000 with the estate taking back a $900,000 mortgage at 1 percent over prime float, for ten years.

To help with the mortgage payments the property was rented from time to time for $2,000 a day to studios for filming and to celebrities like Paul McCartney for parties.

Within the year, it was up for sale again at $4 million; the Iranians had already turned down $3.5 million. "With $700,000 down," Stan Herman said, "the Iranians were able to quadruple their equity in less than a year. That's leverage!"

Tony Curtis, like agent Jane Jones, knows about leverage. Nine years ago he bought the Keck estate for $300,000, putting up approximately $25,000 in actual cash. Five years later he sold it to Sonny and Cher for $950,000. That's leverage too!

2. DEPRECIATION.

"Of all the advantages of owning real estate," said commercial-industrial Realtor Jan Campbell, "depreciation is the most beneficial."

Bronzed and attractive, thirty-three-year-old Jan sat in her Honolulu office in a long Hawaiian print dress and explained that depreciation is another name for tax shelter. "If an investor, for instance, built a brick building at a cost of $100,000 and used the government's declining balance method of depreciation, the first full year's depreciation allowance would be $3,750. (Depending on remaining years of useful life.) In other words," she said, "the first $3,750 the investor received from his building would not be taxed."

"Suppose the property doesn't depreciate—suppose it increases in value?"

"It makes no difference. As a matter of fact, property

hasn't depreciated in one-hundred years. Look what's happened here in Honolulu while investors were taking their depreciation allowance."

The blonde Miss Campbell, president of Jan Campbell, Inc., occupies a suite of offices at 32 Merchant Street in a building once described as the handsomest in Honolulu. Now in the process of being restored, the building offers rental space in the opulent atmosphere of copper-trimmed doors and windows, marble stairways, deep-pile carpeting and imported antiques, at $2.00 a square foot. Built in 1910 at a cost of $160,000 it will cost at least that much to restore the building today, and much more to accomplish the adoptive uses—restaurant and office space. Jan's firm, composed of three equally attractive female associates in their twenties, serves as leasing agent for 32 Merchant Street.

"If the owners of this building," Jan said, "had a 100 percent mortgage and none of the money in the building was, in a strict sense, theirs, they could take the depreciation allowance on the full amount. The land underneath is not depreciable, of course. In other words, they would not deduct solely on the amount of their own money invested.

"And that's another example of leverage too," she added.

Jan has been in commercial-industrial brokerage since 1972. "There were only two women in the field at that time in Hawaii. There are only seven or eight now."

When I asked her background, she replied: "I majored in English Literature and Journalism at the University of Hawaii."

"No business courses?"

"None. I thought figures were a bore until I got into real estate. Now I'm hooked on them. This business will do that for a woman."

Robert Bruss explains depreciation as a noncash tax deduction to give the property owner a tax-free return of his capital as the real estate (or personal property) improvements wear out or become obsolete. All real and personal property can be depreciated on a straight-line basis for a fixed dollar amount each year of its estimated remaining useful life.

Robert Bruss takes a hypothetical income property investment, such as apartments, stores, or offices, and gives some possible leverage alternatives and their results:

| Cash Down Payment (Equity) | $100,000 100% | $50,000 50% | $40,000 40% | $30,000 30% | $25,000 25% | $20,000 20% | $10,000 10% |
|---|---|---|---|---|---|---|---|
| Annual Mortgage Payment (30 yr. 9-1/2%) | 0 | 5,045 | 6,054 | 7,063 | 7,568 | 8,072 | 9,081 |
| Minus Annual Interest (Tax Deductible) | 0 | 4,745 | 5,694 | 6,643 | 7,118 | 7,592 | 8,541 |
| Annual Equity Mortgage Build-up (First Year) | 0 | 300 | 360 | 420 | 450 | 480 | 540 |
| Annual Net Cash Spendable | 10,000 | 4,955 | 3,946 | 2,937 | 2,432 | 1,928 | 919 |
| Depreciation $80,000 Building Value 125% Method (First Year) | 5,000 | 5,000 | 5,000 | 5,000 | 5,000 | 5,000 | 5,000 |
| Taxable Income (or Loss) | 5,000 | 255 | [694] | [1,643] | [2,118] | [2,592] | [3,541] |
| Tax Shelter (Tax Free Income) | 5,000 | 4,700 | 4,640 | 4,580 | 4,550 | 4,520 | 4,460 |
| RETURN ON CASH DOWN PAYMENT, IN RELATION TO: | | | | | | | |
| Annual Net Spendable Cash | 10% | 9.9% | 9.9% | 9.8% | 9.7% | 9.6% | 9.2% |
| Annual Equity Build-up as % of Down Payment (First Year) | 0 | .6% | .9% | 1.4% | 1.8% | 2.4% | 5.4% |
| Total Return on Investment | 10% | 10.5% | 10.8% | 11.2% | 11.5% | 12.0% | 14.6% |

(PLUS INCOME TAX PAYMENT SAVINGS DUE TO TAX LOSS)

"The estimated value of the land is $20,000, and that's nondeductible?" I asked.

"Yes, and we're basing it on an estimated useful life of twenty years."

## Opportunities in HUD and savings and loan properties.

Each month at the close of the last business day, the Department of Housing and Urban Development in cities throughout the country prepares an inventory of all repossessed properties. This inventory is duplicated and distributed to all registered brokers. In the course of business during the month, updated information is published and mailed out to brokers.

Savings and loan institutions will provide a list of owners in default to brokers who wish to subscribe to the service. Notices of default of savings and loan properties are posted at the county courthouse for ninety days, and are advertised for twenty-one days in a public place. If the property in default is in the posting stage, you can go directly to the owners with an offer for their equity. If your offer is accepted, you can pick up the back payments, and the property is yours.

Zoe Huntsinger obtained her California broker's license in 1960 and has used it almost exclusively for her own investments, concentrating on low-income properties (single family and multiple dwellings, up to twenty-five units). About one-fourth of the sixty-odd properties bought have been retained for investment purposes; the other 75 percent were refurbished to meet FHA and VA standards and resold.

"There are greater opportunities in savings and loan than in the HUD properties," she said. "Sometimes a company will facilitate a loan so that I can get in for a dollar down."

"What makes a property a good candidate for refurbishing?"

"A sound structure. You can replace roofs; you can always change electrical circuiting to meet present-day standards; recarpet, retile, paint, correct dry rot, etc. But the basic structure of the house must be sound."

The amount of time taken to get a house back on the market depends, she explained, on how extensive the repairs needed.

"A property should be bought, repaired, put on the market, and sold within 120 days. But to turn property over that quickly you must stay in the lower price range."

"How low?"

"The top price would be $35,000. Anything above that figure limits your clientele."

Most defaulted or repossessed houses, she said, fall into the $15,000 to $20,000 price range—sometimes higher. "But I've bought houses for $5,000."

"What's the first step after you receive a HUD listing of repossessed properties?"

"First step is to take a look at the neighborhood. If there are too many boarded-up houses in the area, you can't sell the property no matter how good it is—or how good you make it.

"If the neighborhood looks all right, I take a look inside. I take a pad with me and make a list of everything that needs to be done—windows replaced, toilet replaced (these are often stolen and used for planters, there's no accounting for taste). Sometimes the walls have been so badly damaged that they have to be paneled (the most economical and aesthetic way to correct this kind of damage). Sometimes the hot water tank is old and must be replaced. Of course, 95 percent of the homes must be repainted, inside and out. When I get home, I sit down and figure what it's going to cost me to have it repaired and what it'll cost to sell it. Unless I can see at least three thousand dollars profit in a property needing extensive repairs, I dismiss it as a possible investment."

She occasionally runs across a house that needs no repairs, she said. In one instance, she bought a defaulted house for $11,879 by paying $100 down to a savings and loan institution, picked up two months' back rent of $250, and sold the house two weeks later for $14,500.

Some HUD properties are "all cash," she said, but explained: "I get a signature loan from the bank, repayable in 90 days, and leave my own funds intact. The costs of repairs are paid from my own personal checking account and after all repairs are completed and the house sold, I make a demand on the escrow company for total amount of repairs, requesting that the check be made to my personal account. This way it does not come in as capital gain."

There are, of course, other ways to handle the transaction—depending on the individual's tax structure.

Some women brokers and agents interested in refurbishing and retaining foreclosed properties are taking advantage of the government's Leased Housing Program for low-income families. This relieves an owner of the triple necessity of collecting rents, evicting tenants, and paying for tenant-inflicted damage to her property.

The Leased Housing Program is administered by the federal government through the Department of Housing and Urban Development, which provides annual financial contributions to city housing authorities throughout the country to carry out the program by means of an Annual Contributions Contract.

Agent Jane Doe learned that a savings and loan institution in her city was foreclosing a property consisting of six two-bedroom units. Agent Jane gave the lending institution $1.00 down and they made a "loan to facilitate" for $25,000. She then refurbished the building, repaired all walls, put on a new roof, eliminated all signs of dry rot, repaired front porch, painted exterior and interior, and installed six refrigerated air conditioning units, six new refrigerators and six new stoves. Total cost of preparing the six units to meet Housing Authority standards was $10,000. The savings and loan institution then made a permanent loan of $25,000 on the property, and placed a $35,000 market value on it.

Jane then leased the six units to the Housing Authority in her city for $576 a month on a five-year lease, subject to renewal for an additional term of five years beyond the first term and for subsequent terms of like tenure.

On the first day of each calendar month during the term of the lease, the Housing Authority deposits a check for $576 to the account Jane has set up for the property.

Purpose of the lease, as stated in standard lease form is to provide decent, safe, and sanitary housing for eligible low-income families in accordance with the Housing Authority program.

The Housing Authority pays for gas and electricity (collected from tenants), and Owner Jane provides and pays for water, sewer, and garbage service. Jane makes all structural and exterior repairs, including plumbing, heating equipment, and electrical wiring. She also keeps in repair any other equipment she supplies or provides in the terms of her lease. The authority, through its tenants, is liable to Jane for any damage to the premises beyond ordinary wear and tear, and the authority will pay any property tax increase up to, but not to exceed, 20 percent of the base year taxes during the initial term of the lease and any renewal thereof.

|  |  | Annual |
|---|---|---|
| Income: $576 per month = $576 × 12 = $6,912.00 | | $6,912.00 |
| Expenditures: | | |
| Monthly payment on $25,000 loan | | |
| @ 6-3/4% (including taxes and insurance) | | |
| $296.50 × 12 | $3,558.00 | |
| Garbage Pickup @ $20.00 per mo. | 240.00 | |
| Water and Sewer @ $45.00 per mo. | 540.00 | |
| Estimated Normal Maintenance Cost | 323.00 | |
| Total Expenditures | | 4,661.00 |
| NET ANNUAL INCOME ON $10,000 INVESTED | | $2,251.00 |
| (Plus equity build-up and tax shelter set up on 12-year straightline depreciation.) | | |

"When you buy and repair, you're your own boss," an agent-investor in a city termed "distressed" by the Housing Authority said.

"Maybe I like it because I'm a gambler at heart—maybe because I relate better to men. At any rate, it's a great career for the woman who is turned-off by the idea of chauffeuring another woman around while she vacillates between buying the house with the green tile in the bathroom or the house with the yellow tile in the kitchen.

"That's the fantastic thing about this business. It allows a woman to find her own thing—then do her own thing."

## Money-making opportunities in the affluent suburbs.

"Sometimes," an agent in one of San Francisco's upper-income suburbs said, "you'll run across a property that's been on the market for months. Maybe all it needs is a good paint job to make it sell. Or maybe the carpeting is so worn that it turns people off, or the owners have left frayed drapes at the windows. Many clients can't see hidden possibilities, and after a property sits too long, salespeople, as well as clients, begin to shy away from it. But with a structurally sound house in a stable neighborhood, plus a little imagination— you've got a financial winner."

Her detailed account of her first venture into buying and refurbishing an unwanted property should appeal to anyone unable to resist a challenge.

"It was a large home, four bedrooms, three baths, living room, two family rooms, kitchen but no dining room. It was in an excellent neighborhood, and was about five years old. It looked fifty in terms of wear and tear.

"When the owners, a doctor and his wife, separated, the wife evidently was awarded the furniture and the husband the children."

The father and children "batched it" for several months in the denuded house, she said—the teenage boy doing the cooking, while according to neighbors the doctor practiced his guitar on the redwood deck stretching across the back of the house. When the family moved to another state, the house sat on the market vacant for almost a year. The owners overlooked the importance of leaving the house clean, and over the months the closed off premises took on a soured, unpleasant odor.

"That odor hit you in the face the moment you opened the front door—another reason why agents began bypassing it with their clients.

"A competent listing agent would have advised the owner on the importance of leaving the house immaculate, and if the owner didn't heed the advice, the agent would have had the place cleaned, and paid for it—if unable to collect from the owner.

"The house had so many unattractive features that agents and clients forgot that it was a large sound home in an upper-income neighborhood—priced below its sometimes smaller, but well-kept neighbors. One of the many features that turned buyers off was the fact that when you opened the front door you looked directly into the kitchen, and in addition you were confronted by four separate floor styles, without moving an inch. You stood on 12" squares of black and white vinyl in the entry hall; looked into the living room at extra width, pegged hardwood flooring; to conventional 3" hardwood flooring in the hallway and on the stairs, and into the kitchen at still another jarringly bright vinyl pattern. Two bedrooms had been painted a violent pink; another was a nondescript, marred yellow, and the fourth, a bilious green—adorned with psychedelic wall murals in purple and black. Frayed drapes sagged dejectedly at all the windows, as if they, too, had given up on the house. The kids had punched holes in the wall in one of the closets, but other than that the walls were intact. The stove was a nightmare, the oven so black with burned grease that it looked inoperable, the burners in the same condition."

She made a low offer, she said. The absentee-owner came back with a counter, and she accepted.

"First thing I did was take down the old dusty drapes and sell them to a second-hand dealer. The only structural change I made was the addition of a wall in the large kitchen-family room area. The room was immense (approximately 20 by 24) so we still had space for a breakfast area in the kitchen. Separating that huge room gave us a beautiful 12 by 14 carpeted formal dining room, opening off the living room and with double glass doors (already in) leading to the redwood deck. A single door led from the kitchen to the deck also, so access to and from the kitchen was no problem. I also had an attractive, louvered door put in between the kitchen and entry hall so that you did not look directly into the kitchen.

"After the holes in the closet had been repaired, and the interior walls painted in off-white, we solved the problem of the four different flooring styles by carpeting the entire house, except for the kitchen (adding an area rug in the entry hall to cut down on wear and tear).

"We put the house back on the market, with the exterior painted and the landscaping pruned to perfection. The windows were clean but undraped, the holes in the closet had been repaired, the oven and burners were in immaculate condition. We priced it at $10,000 above my total cost—including repairs, interest on loan, fire and liability insurance, prorated taxes, closing costs, and estimated cost of selling. Since we were in a neighborhood of homes where the price was not out of line, it sold within a month.

"The entire transaction from opening of escrow, through repairs, to sale and close of new escrow, took seven months. I had made $10,000 and I had the added satisfaction of taking an unwanted property and turning it into something highly desirable.

"This business," she said, "can be mind-expanding in so many ways. That first venture made me aware of how little I knew about design, color, etc. While some of my friends were studying finance, real estate law, tax, etc., I enrolled for courses in interior design in one of our local colleges."

These courses, she said, have been of inestimable help. "I've made many sales because I was able to tell clients how to make a house more to their taste, if they fell in love with the exterior or the setting, but could not abide some of the interior's shortcomings."

She then enrolled in a contractor's licensing course. "I may decide to take the test some day, but for now I'm content to know what that contractor who is giving me a bid is talking about. I run across an average of two 'sleepers' a year—houses I can buy, repair, or sometimes just redecorate, and make a nice profit."

Another agent with similar interests has opened an interior design studio in partnership with a young graduate AID and now handles clients' needs for carpets, drapes, wallpaper, and furniture through her own firm.

## But suppose we have a depression?

For unabashedly frank answers to this and other questions I set up an appointment with the anonymous "Mona," whose specialty is real estate investment and who practices what she preaches. Her first investment was made in 1966, the year she received her license (a single-family dwelling in a low-risk rental area). In the intervening years she has invested in two duplexes, a fifteen-unit apartment building, a seventy-thousand-square-foot warehouse, and a five-story business building.

"Is real estate as good an investment as the professionals tell us?"

"Hell, do you know anyone today who would sell their home for what they paid for it?"

"If depreciation is the great advantage you people selling investment real estate claim, why isn't it mentioned in most investment books?"

"If the so-called investment book doesn't cover real estate, what's to mention? This is the only investment that's depreciable. Stocks certainly aren't."

"But even with depreciation or tax shelter, doesn't an investor eventually pay the tax when he sells?"

"A portion, of course. But in the meantime your investor has had the earnings from tax-sheltered or depreciated monies that otherwise would have been paid as income tax. As a matter of fact, many investors arrange a tax-deferred exchange rather than selling."

Tax-deferred exchange, she explained, means that property held for investment, or used in the investor's trade or business, may be exchanged for property of equal or greater value, provided the new property is also to be held for that purpose. There is no capital gain, and a series of tax-deferred exchanges may avoid a sale for a lifetime.

"But the investor's heirs would have to pay the taxes."

"No, except for estate and inheritance taxes, the investor's heirs receive the property tax-free. And the basis from which they begin depreciation is the fair market value at the time of the inheritance. (Determined by an appraisal.) In other words, after the investor has taken all of the depreciation out of a series of investments, investor's heirs start over—based on current values and without paying capital gains tax on the value increase."

"You mean an investor can pyramid real estate holdings without paying capital gains tax, depreciate everything to the fullest extent possible, and then his heirs are allowed to do the same thing again?"

"Right!"

"Why doesn't everyone exchange properties that have risen in value rather than selling them and reinvesting the proceeds?"

"Some taxpayers are in such high brackets that they prefer to pay taxes at capital gains rates in order to get higher depreciation deductions. But it's a damn shame that some ordinary investors sell every year, pay their capital gains and reinvest what's left, without knowing that their entire equity could have been transferred into another property without paying a penny in capital gains taxes.

"Tax-free exchange," she added, "is a right real estate investors alone have. It does not apply to dealers."

"What's the difference in a dealer and an investor?"

"More than five transactions a year puts you in the dealer category."

"What about the 'trials of management'? That seems to be one of the arguments against real estate investing."

"Real estate management firms offer headache-proof service. The investor should include their fee among projected expenses when evaluating the investment."

"How does real estate compare with life insurance as an investment?"

"Hell. Insurance companies use the premiums paid by their policy holders to invest in real estate!

"But," she added quickly, "everyone should have enough insurance to avoid hardship in case of death. And for God's sake, I don't mean that a woman should sell her home and buy investment properties. The equity in her home is as good as cash in the bank."

"But is it wise for a woman to borrow money in order to invest?"

"We'd all die of old age if we waited until we could pay cash in this day and age."

"Suppose we have a depression?? What happens to our real estate investments?"

"I know people who've waited forty years for another depression so they can, quote, 'Pick up property cheap.' And I know a woman whose carefully guarded nest egg has shrunk so in the inflated atmosphere it wouldn't make a decent omelette; and an elderly couple whose guaranteed retirement income from his life insurance plan will now guarantee them moving expenses to the nearest subsidized housing development.

"Seriously," she said, "in the unlikely event of a full-scale depression, cash would, of course, increase in purchasing power, and prices on everything would fall—groceries, clothes, stocks, and cars. Real estate too—temporarily. Inevitably, as the population increases, demand will increase, and we can make more cornflakes, cars, television sets, shoes—just about anything to keep up with the demand. The point to remember is that we *can't make land*. Real estate is a limited commodity. In plain English—there'll never be any more of it!"

# CHAPTER 8

# International Sales —
# "Not for Men Only"

*American property has stood the
test of time, like no other investment
in the world.*

### Femininity plus expertise.

"Femininity and expertise are a powerful combination," according to John Hunsinger, president of an Atlanta commercial-industrial firm. He referred to Rose Marie Garrison, his Far East specialist. The Hunsinger firm, with a representative in Tokyo, and in partnership with the French firm Cabinet Augusts Thouard, is one of a growing number of American firms active in international sales. Rose Marie (R.M. on her cards) has been responsible for locating Yashica, Hitachi America, Hitachi Shibaden, Kanpai, Noritaki, and Kawasaki in Atlanta.

"My transactions run $30,000 to $500,000," Rose Marie said. "And I average fifteen to twenty a year."

"GERMANS LIKE HOUSTON," "EMPIRE STATE BUILDING IMPRESSES JAPANESE," "NEW IRISH-AMERICAN TIE-UP," "INDIANS TO ROCKEFELLER CENTER," "$40 MILLION CANADIAN DEAL," "BRITISH BUILDER IN AMERICA," "KOREANS

MAKE SUCCESS OF NEW YORK BUILDING," "WEST GERMAN
CONSORTIUM PAYS $92.5 MILLION FOR 80% INTEREST IN
HOUSTON OFFICE COMPLEX," "BELGIAN INVESTS $7 MIL-
LION IN SOUTH TEXAS RANCH." American real estate tops
the shopping lists of European, Asian, South American,
and Middle East investors. The big institutions, such as
banks and pension funds, are buying primarily new
skyscrapers and regional shopping malls. Wealthy individuals are usually looking for smaller commercial
and industrial properties costing between $100,000 and
$1 million.

## Why they're buying American.

Listed below are some of the advantages foreign investors find in American real estate.

*Political stability.* America has it. Many other countries do not, and it is a characteristic highly conducive to
long-term investments such as real estate.

*A reservoir of professional expertise.* America boasts
more qualified property people to manage real estate
investments than can be found anywhere else in the
world.

*The low cost of land.* By comparison with most other
developed countries, America has a tremendous
amount of relatively cheap acreage—an especially attractive asset to foreigners in whose countries building
land is in short supply.

*The ease of communication.* Technologically and
linguistically, America is nearly ideal. The phone system is excellent, and English is considered the universal
language of business.

*A tax system favorable to real estate investment.* This
is difficult for some Americans to believe—but ask your
foreign investors.

*Less restrictive immigration laws.* In case the overseas investor wants to relocate, our laws are less restrictive than those of many other countries.

*An open economy.* Until the extent of overseas fundings becomes much greater, this country will probably remain an open economy (unlike Canada and many other countries where economic nationalism is in full flower).

*A free currency exchange policy.* Getting money out of American investments is easy contrasted to getting money out of investments in many other countries. (In some, it is almost impossible.)

*The ease of transferring ownership.* It is far less difficult to transfer ownership in this country than in most others.

*Minimal expropriation risk.* Aside from carefully circumscribed laws of eminent domain, the foreign investor has little need to worry about having his American real estate suddenly taken over by the government—as in revolution-prone nations.

*Secure frontiers.* Foreign investors feel that if any country is likely *not* to be overrun by a foreign military power, it's the United States.

*A huge and diverse real estate market.* An important plus for the foreign investor when he is buying or selling.

*A sound legal system.* America's legal system is established and predictable. Not only are personal and property rights constitutionally guaranteed, but there is also a wide acceptance of title insurance.

*Accounting standards.* Professional, well-established auditing techniques are supported by strict legal procedures.

*Moderate property use restrictions.* Though they are somewhat restrictive in comparison to earlier practices in most parts of the country, they are far less harsh than in some other parts of the world.

*Personal safety*. Despite crime in the streets in many American cities, there is little fear of abductions, riots, etc.—common occurrences in certain nations.

*Appreciation*. Appreciation of property has been better historically in America than in any other country.

*The availability of finance*. America is probably unsurpassed for the variety and extent of debt financing capabilities. And it offers the unique feature of "leverage."

*A hedge against inflation*. American property has stood the test of time, like no other investment. Sophisticated foreign investors are well aware of this.

John Hunsinger of Atlanta summed up the attitude of foreign investors with: "In short, no matter how much we Americans complain and criticize—the foreign investor obviously has confidence in the stability of American properties and the American government.

"They see other governments—including their own—going more and more to the socialistic system. For instance, it may take two years or more to get ready to develop a property in France—because of the huge amount of paperwork involved. The number of approvals needed before you can tear down a five-hundred-year-old building in Paris in mind-boggling. In Atlanta, it takes thirty days to do what it could take two years to do in Western European countries.

"In Japan, face is very important—who you are—who you know. You can spend three months on the preliminaries of drinking tea and attending meetings. They are shocked at the speed with which we put together a transaction.

"We have a representative in Tokyo, Tadao Shimizu. If a Tokyo or Yokohama firm is interested in space in this country, Mr. Shimizu sends the information to Rose Marie. If they want to locate in the southeastern part of the country, she handles it. If in another section—New York, San Francisco—we go through SIR" (Society of Industrial Realtors, 430 North Michigan Avenue, Chicago, Illinois 60611).

"One week from the time Rose Marie receives the request, she can telephone Tokyo and give Mr. Shimizu guaranteed rates on office or warehouse space anywhere in the United States or Canada—based on the Japanese firm's specifications.

"A transaction that might take two years to complete in Japan, takes from three to six months to complete here. They like our way of doing business—but they don't understand it."

## Making it big in international sales.

Is there a place for you in international sales? Or is it an area dominated by supermales, where a woman risks losing limb and income by attempting to put a foot in a foreign door? The key word is, again, education!

Ebby Halliday of Dallas, active in the American Chapter, International Real Estate Federation, is selling American residential properties to foreign nationals from Saudi Arabia, Germany, Japan, and Belgium. "I have brochures going out to twenty-two of the thirty-five member countries of the federation covering residences in Dallas selling in excess of a million dollars," she said. Sally Goodale, of Scottsdale and Phoenix, a director of the International Federation, is selling Arizona residential properties and land to foreign investors. Alice Mason is leasing and selling in New York, Bernice Rappaport in Beverly Hills, Ruth Johnston on the San Francisco Peninsula, Myra Fisher in Honolulu,

Jeanne Begg and Joan Day in Washington, D.C.

Basalle Wong of San Francisco's Geary Street makes a twice yearly trip to Hong Kong and Taipei—more frequently, if necessary—to service overseas buyers. She thumbed through an album filled with pictures of apartment houses, warehouses, office buildings, restaurants, industrial complexes and shopping malls. Twenty units on Balboa for $360,000, twelve units for $300,000. An office building for $1.4 million. Warehouse, $100,000. Six units, $200,000, six more in a less desirable area for $72,000. The album contained information on seventy-six properties altogether.

"Are these the properties you will take to Hong Kong and Taipei to show on your next trip?"

"These are the properties I have sold," she said.

Stockbrokers, contractors, businessmen and bankers in Hong Kong and Taipei are investing in the San Francisco area.

"Most buy without seeing the property," she said in halting English. "They know I know the market, and I tell the truth. Sometimes they write and say a friend has told them about me, and say they have $100,000 or $200,000 to invest. And, 'What can you find for me? What is best for me?' they say."

She pointed to a listing, a six-unit apartment building in the Richmond district. She bought it, she said, for an investor for $172,000. Three years later she sent him an offer for $300,000, but he did not want to sell. Sometimes her investor sells—still without seeing his property—and she reinvests the money for him.

"What are they looking for—what type investment?"

"The Chinese like industrial or commercial for income, over apartment houses."

If she is unable to find a suitable property for an overseas buyer, she negotiates for land and contracts with a builder for a warehouse, an apartment building, or an office complex. Her most ambitious project to date concerns the acquisition of a tract of land near San Francisco's International Airport for development by a Hong Kong hotelman.

Her international sales usually run, she said, from $100,000 to $1 million. Her highest was a block of industrial property for $1.5 million to a Hong Kong investor. She has submitted an offer for $6 million for a San Francisco property.

Eleven years ago, Basalle Wong was tending a tiny grocery store on Geary Street, while her four children did their homework in a back room. "One of my customers was a broker. He told me I should go to school and get a real estate license."

Rose Marie Garrison came into international commercial-industrial real estate through the secretarial route. "I was working for an excellent commercial-industrial firm. I saw what the men were making. One day I got hungry."

In addition to locating numerous Japanese firms in Atlanta, Rose Marie also works with her firm's consultant in Europe.

"Is it more difficult to work with foreign buyers?" I asked.

"Yes. For instance, I was totally unfamiliar with the Japanese culture. I had to learn something about them—how they think, how they operate, their customs. Then there's the language barrier, too."

Until they met Rose Marie, unenlightened Japanese businessmen thought that the entrance of a woman into a room meant one of two things—time to eat, or time for entertainment. Understandably, they were reluctant to conduct business with the attractive, dark-haired, green-eyed Rose Marie. "They could not comprehend that a pretty young woman was competent to handle their business affairs," said John Hunsinger, head of her firm, "but, this image changed after a few minutes in her presence."

The Hunsinger firm was responsible for bringing the Kanpai Restaurant to Atlanta. At the opening cocktail party, attended by a number of Japanese businessmen, John Hunsinger searched for a way to introduce his Far East representative. "I decided to introduce her as a 'powerful woman.' "

"From that night on," Rose Marie said "I have been introduced by the Japanese to one another as 'a powerful woman.' "

"Are all your buyers men?"

"All of them. Once a Japanese man is confident you know what you're doing they'll stay with you, give you total loyalty and trust. I enjoy working with them very much."

## How to break in.

Should you pack your bag after the state notifies you that you have passed the real estate examination; pause long enough to affiliate with a broker and gather up a few of his listings; buy a new suit; board the next plane to Paris; take a suite at the Ritz; dine at the most expensive restaurants—and get on the phone (in English, of course) to arrange appointments with banks and investment groups? Have you thought of a career in foundation garments?

If you are thinking of a future in international sales, your number one priority should be a broker's license. Whether you eventually open your own firm or place your license with another broker, the added knowledge is a must for international sales. Affiliation with a broker with an established reputation in international sales will give you the opportunity to learn the intricacies of foreign investment while providing a forum to successfully complete transactions. Proficiency in one or more foreign languages should be high on your list as preparation for international sales. While most investors speak some English, the professional fluent in an investor's native tongue is certainly at an advantage—psychologically and practically—over Mary English-only. Or John English-only! If you plan to specialize in a particular country, study its cultural history and business methods. Spend your next vacation there. Foreign investors are sophisticated and knowledgeable in the ways of finance and inflation. A high-pressure pitch by Joan Yokel involving a series of complicated legal maneuvers—made more difficult to understand because she has sprinkled it liberally with colloquialisms—is highly offensive to the foreign investor and apt to drive him and his money into the arms of another country.

Licensed real estate women, fluent in any foreign language—and especially those with the added advantage of the cultural heritage—should consider education looking toward international sales.

Membership in the American Chapter of the International Real Estate Federation (FIABCI—the initials of the original French organization) is another essential step for the woman interested in the international market. Membership is open to all members of the National Association of Realtors.

FIABCI was officially founded in Paris in 1951 by five countries: Austria, Belgium, the Federal Republic of Germany, France and the United States of America. Today it has a membership of thirty countries, with fifty-nine professional organizations in Europe, Africa,

America, Asia and Australia—grouping over six-hundred-thousand real estate professionals. Twenty-two corresponding countries maintain regular relationships with FIABCI.

Objectives of the international organization are the study of all aspects of major problems with which the real estate profession is concerned in each country; the pooling and circulation of general and technical information to facilitate professional and public action; the protection of members' interests, and assistance to members whenever the rules of the real estate profession are called into question; vocational training for the young, and extension of their knowledge through international exchanges of trainees; and the unification and development of real estate policy throughout the world—publicity and communication techniques, town planning and new social patterns.

Headquarters of the federation have been in Paris since the founding. The four official languages are English, French, German, and Spanish.

Since 1954, FIABCI has had consultative status as a nongovernmental organization with the Committee of Housing, Building and Planning of the Economic Commission for Europe under the United Nations Economic and Social Council. It has a permanent representative with that body in Geneva and is also represented at various meetings and seminars throughout the world.

In 1964, a permanent secretariat was established in Brussels to undertake studies of the right to practice the profession of real estate agent as part of the right to set up in business. Every year FIABCI representatives are invited to briefing sessions at the Brussels Headquarters of the European Community.

A magazine in four languages, the *FIABCI-Reporter*,

is published quarterly, containing information about real estate business throughout the world, accounts of the various activities of the federation, and technical essays on various aspects of the real estate profession.

The FIABCI roster contains nearly six-thousand names of real estate professionals in all the member countries in alphabetical and geographical order with the address, telephone number, and branches in which they specialize—an invaluable tool in the development of international professional contacts.

Among the FIABCI publications are: *The Real Estate Glossary* (in four languages); *The Real Estate Vocabulary* (in six languages); *The Real Estate Guide* (in four languages); *Incorporated Companies* (a survey of the legislation in fourteen countries); and *Twenty Years of International Life (1948–1968)*.

Ruth Johnston of Burlingame, California, has located homes in Europe for several American buyers, and believes contacts made through FIABCI are invaluable. During a recent FIABCI meeting held in San Francisco, she took six Australians, active in the residential market, on a tour of Bay Area single-family homes. "I brought them back to my home for cocktails," she said.

"When I was in Madrid, I was entertained by a Spanish broker in the condominium market, and was given the opportunity to represent two condominium projects—one in Madrid, and one in Switzerland."

In addition to the contacts you will make, attendance at an annual International Congress, hosted by one of the member chapters, enables you to hear top authorities from various countries. You may participate in work programs regarding real estate development, sales, management, and financing throughout the world. Recent meetings have been held in Lucerne, Mexico City, Paris, San Francisco, and Amsterdam.

## Summing it up.

The essential step toward a career in the international market is affiliation with a firm doing business in that area. But, a representative of Mr. International Sales will not be standing outside your home, contract in hand, the day the postman brings word that you have passed your state exam. Neither will he drop to his knees a few years later to urge that you give up your successful three-bedroom, two-bath career, marry him, and live happily ever after in international sales.

The woman interested in a career in international sales must prove to her chosen broker that she has something to offer him—and his buyers: A proven real estate track record in domestic sales of like properties. Proficiency in one or more foreign languages. Knowledge of the culture and business methods of a country or countries. And, a desire to learn! learn! learn!

# CHAPTER 9

## Selling the Celebrities

*$600,000 down, $1,800 a month payments,
and $24,000 a year property taxes.*

Can a redheaded nurse from a small New Zealand town find happiness selling homes in Beverly Hills? Margot Faustbiender has.

"Sometimes I pinch myself to make sure it's really true," she said in high-pitched, clipped English. "I made more than the prime minister of New Zealand last year."

Margot is associated with the Mike Silverman agency, and is selling properties in an area where a house may be leased for $7,500 a month; two-bedroom condominiums sell for $300,000, and price tags may begin at half a million and escalate to three million; where beachfront property in the famed Malibu colony is up to $2,500 a front foot, and sea- and sun-weathered shacks on forty- or fifty-foot lots start at $250,000; where the homes must be fit for such clients as Elizabeth Taylor, Dino de Laurentiis, Charles Bronson, Cher Bono, Frank Sinatra, or a princess—the sister of the Shah of Iran.

In one year, the Silverman firm sold $30,000,000 worth of homes in the top-of-the-line areas of Beverly

Hills, Bel Air, Holmby Hills, Westwood, and Brentwood—with an occasional sale in Acapulco or Palm Springs.

Associate Julie York, ex-actress-model, sold over $1.5 million in Beverly Hills real estate in one week. Ruth Hoffman sold five properties for an amount approaching $2 million in two weeks. In her eight years with the firm, Ruth has sold an average of twenty-eight silk-stocking homes a year. Jane Lewis had sales of $6.4 million one year, involving a total of twenty-nine homes. She had sales in six months in excess of $5 million—and had thirteen homes in escrow at one time, one for $400,000 and the other twelve all over $150,000!

*A millionaire for every property—somewhere.*

Josephine Schaefer of New York, one of the outstanding veteran women of the industry, was probably the first woman involved in the sale of property to a well-known figure.

In 1930, she received a call from a man who said he was staying at the Plaza, wanted to rent a three-room furnished apartment for $125 a month—and his name was Paul Getty.

Jo Schaefer showed her famous prospect three-room apartments, six-room apartments, eight, twelve. None would do. She finally placed him in a fifteen-room furnished apartment for $15,000 a year. When the lease was up a year later, she contacted him about renewing. "Instead of renewing the lease, I'll just buy the building," said Mr. Getty.

Some time later, he again telephoned Jo Schaefer. He wanted, he said, to buy a New York building as an investment.

Evidencing the audacity that has carried women to the top of the business, she immediately suggested the

Empire State Building. Unfortunately, the Empire State was too big—even for Paul Getty. She next mentioned the Hotel Pierre—without the slightest idea whether the hotel was for sale at any price. Getty seemed interested, and she talked the owners of the Pierre into listing it—at what she considered a good investment for Getty. Getty agreed with her judgment, and the transaction was closed—a multi-million dollar sale in the depths of the Depression.

"Howard Hughes was as eccentric about his real estate transactions—as some other aspects of his life," said California broker Ruth Johnston. "I located properties for him on several different occasions—each transaction fell through because of impossible demands made by the man.

"During the forties he became interested in a house in Santa Monica owned by a Swiss client of mine. She returned to Switzerland for a part of each year, and I leased the house for her. She always locked off her master bedroom.

"Hughes wanted the master bedroom, and he gave me forty-eight hours to get it unlocked. I cabled my client's attorney in Paris, but she had just left. I called Lucerne, to learn that she was traveling. Her staff would try to reach her. A few hours after Mr. Hughes's deadline, she called from somewhere in Europe saying that she was agreeable to giving Mr. Hughes access to the master bedroom. I contacted Mr. Hughes's representative. He called back and informed me that Mr. Hughes wanted no part of it. We were two hours past his deadline.

"Another time, I made arrangements for him to lease a home from a couple with a sixteen-year-old daughter. Hughes kept erratic hours. He rang the doorbell of the home at 12:30 A.M., and when the sixteen-year-old opened the door, she was met with, 'I'm Howard

Hughes. I'd like to look at the house now.' The girl explained that her parents were out, that she would call them, and they'd be there in five or ten minutes."

Hughes looked at his watch, and announced: "I'll give them six minutes to get here."

When the owners did not appear in six minutes, he walked away and cancelled the lease the following day.

"My parents drove up as he turned the corner," the girl told Ruth.

Overnight successes in sports, the entertainment field (rock stars, television personalities), or executives of new-growth companies account for most of the "Sold American" expensive properties, according to Bruce Wennerstrom. Mr. Wennerstrom is president of Previews, Inc., a forty-five-year-old company headquartered in Greenwich, Connecticut, specializing in expensive properties needing broad exposure. Since its founding the company has sold more than $5 billion worth of property.

Clients are charged a retainer fee before Previews lists a property. A brochure is drawn up for each property and distributed to brokers worldwide.

Bob Fawcett, of Previews' regional office in Denver, recalled an heiress who paid Previews $40,000 as a retainer to list a property for $2 million, then took the place off the market when she saw Previews' brochure. "I've fallen in love with it all over again," she said.

Sales to foreigners are soaring, said Bruce Wennerstrom. A twenty-six-room San Francisco residence, its exterior a copy of Le Petit Trianon at Versailles, was sold to the Iranian government; a German couple purchased a Virginia property for $1.2 million; a Japanese industrialist, "who had never been to the United States," bought a huge ranch.

Why? Because, according to Mr. Wennerstrom,

foreign celebrities and millionaires consider American homes in prime areas a safe haven for their money. A German buyer commented that Germany was preceding the United States on the road to socialism by about twenty years. Swedish and Italian buyers have cited a stable political system and a relatively low rate of inflation as reasons for their purchases.

Previews has found there is a millionaire, either foreign or domestic, for every house—for a house in Scottsdale, Arizona, with an indoor skating rink; a castle in Illinois with moat, drawbridge, and knight's hall; a circular-shaped house in Connecticut which rotates at five speeds on the pattern of German battleship gun mechanisms. And Previews found a buyer for a 170-year-old house in New Jersey built with rounded corners so that occupants would not have to worry about "ghosts in the corners." Previews sold the home with the claim that it was ghost-free.

The most expensive properties currently listed by the company are a citrus grove in Florida for $30 million, and the King's Landing development near Hilo, Hawaii, for $18 million. As a general rule they do not list properties under $200,000.

Previews' commission is 6 percent of the selling price. In addition, the individual broker receives a 5 percent commission, bringing the total cost for the seller to 11 percent of sales price. If the property sells for more than $2.5 million, the broker receives only a 2-1/2 percent commission. (Statistics are unavailable on the number of crying towels sold to brokers involved in the company's $2.5 million properties.)

In the early forties, when the company was in its infancy, Ruth Johnston, then involved in expensive properties in Southern California, was approached by a representative of the company with an offer. "He told me I'd have to travel a great deal. I was very young, and the idea of traveling alone was frightening. Women just didn't do it then. I turned him down.

"Women's liberation came along a few years too late," she said with a sigh.

In 1964 Previews requested Myra Fisher, who had been involved with expensive properties in Honolulu and New York and held a broker's license in both states, to come to London for the purpose of selling Grand Bahamas Island.

"How does one get a chance to sell Previews' properties today?" I asked Bob Fawcett.

"Any licensed broker can get on our mailing list," he said. "All he, or she, has to do is write us. We encourage broker participation, in fact we pioneered in this area many years ago."

"Must they have a background in more expensive properties?"

"That's not at all necessary. It's no more difficult to sell a million-dollar property than a $100,000 one. In fact it's sometimes easier because these clients usually don't have to worry about finance."

"Do you have any type training program for brokers interested in selling unusual, expensive properties?"

"No, but we help them. This happened recently. A woman broker had a client who was interested in one of our more expensive properties, and she had never been involved in a sale of this kind before. We pitched in and helped her."

"Any licensed broker," he repeated, "who would like to be on Previews' mailing list need only write and make the request." (Previews, Inc., 51 Weaver St., Greenwich, Connecticut 06830)

"British rock stars and rich Iranians really don't have much in common, except a fondness for expensive homes in Southern California's prestige areas," said Beverly Hills broker and transplanted New York school-teacher June Scott.

"They don't have to worry about financing, they think our high taxes are low, and they like our climate and security. Many of the British rock stars are taxed up to 98 percent of their earned income, so they haven't any alternative but to move from England."

June has sold or leased houses to such stars as Rod Stewart, Elton John, John Lennon, Ringo Starr, etc. "Rock stars tend to get emotional over a house to the point where they want to move in immediately," she said. "They need big houses because they have an army of followers and 'groupies.' Houses in Beverly Hills have such amenities as projection and recording rooms, not to mention pools and tennis courts."

*Wasting your time in three bedrooms and two baths in Harrisburg and Spartanburg?*

Beverly Hills. Douglas Fairbanks paid $35,000 for eleven acres in 1919. In 1978, ex-actress Jody Sherman will show you a one-bedroom condominium on North Oakhurst for $1 million (if it hasn't sold). Condominiums in this building are priced from $750,000 to $1.5 million. Glamorous Elaine Young confides that some clients will pay $100,000 more than a house is worth if it has tennis courts. Beverly Hills High School is considering covering up its oilwells to make room for tennis courts, and the city has passed a law barring presidential helicopter landings.

Should you sell your home, call in a second-hand dealer for the furniture, pack your bag, and take the next Greyhound to the "golden ghetto" to seek fame and fortune—not on the silver screen but in a silver Jaguar, showing homes with show business bloodlines?

Nurse Margot of New Zealand is enamored with picking up the phone and hearing Charles Bronson ask her to show him a home; holding an open house and having Harvey Korman or Orson Welles drop in to follow her into the bedrooms and baths.

But, dark-haired, striking Bernice Rappaport, with the Asher Dann & Frank Jackwerth firm describing selling in Beverly Hills, uses such words as "gut-wrenching," and "heartbreaking."

"Imagine," she said, "what happens to the relationship between two friends when they're both trying to get a listing that may pay them $100,000. I've watched women become emotionally and physically ill in this town.

"This is like no other place in the world. The turnover is incredible. A performer gets a better contract, or is signed for a series, and they have an immediate need to 'move up.' And, if the show is cancelled, or the contract expires, and there's nothing else on the horizon, they move down. I've seen furnishings—pictures, silver, china—everything sold. Six months later maybe something breaks for them, and they're on the phone wanting to 'move up' again.

"But, this does not account for all the turnover," she said. "Properties are increasing in value so rapidly that business managers advise their show business clients here for a short time commitment, to buy a home or condominium rather than rent.

"And, there are the inevitable phonies who spend your time and money looking at homes occupied by Carol Burnett or Elizabeth Taylor, before you learn that they haven't the down payment for a one-room house once occupied by Rin-Tin-Tin.

"It must seem unbelievable to real estate people in

some parts of the country, but it's easier to sell a $300,000 home in this town than a $100,000 one. There are too many people looking for $100,000 homes in Beverly Hills who can't afford them.

"Sometimes your buyers have mafia connections," she ended. "If you don't sell them, someone else will. Gladly!"

Women in the emotion-packed business of selling to the wealthy and powerful, the famous and infamous, advise proceeding with extreme caution in burning your three-bedroom, two-bath bridge in Harrisburg or Spartanburg. Contacts, they point out, are all important. Elaine Young is the daughter-in-law of famed composer Jules Styne, is married to composer Stan Styne, and once was the wife of Gig Young. Julie York is the daughter of a well-known Beverly Hills surgeon, has two brothers involved in real estate—and dates King Faisal's brother. Bernice Rappaport came into real estate with a host of entertainment contacts after several years in television public relations. The wife of a United States senator, or the mother-in-law of a Western European consul is able to meet clients on the social scene. Women whose husbands head firms, or associations; wives of judges, physicians, entertainment or sports celebrities are at an easily understood advantage. If you do not fit into all of the above categories—or even one— think twice, maybe ten times twice—before buying that bus ticket.

"Don't you agree?" I asked nurse Margot, formerly of New Zealand—lately of Beverly Hills.

"Sometimes I have to pinch myself to make sure it's true," she said with a smile. "I made more than the prime minister of New Zealand last year.

"And, Sunday, when I held an open house, I looked up and there standing in the door was ..."

# CHAPTER 10

## How to Go into Business for Yourself

> *Any woman who has a career and a*
> *family develops something in the way*
> *of two personalities. Her problem is to*
> *keep one from draining the life from*
> *the other.*
> Ivy Baker Priest

All a broker ever does," said Eunice Uninformed, "is to
talk on the phone, act like a big wheel, and collect half of
a hard-working agent's commission."

Eunice has had her license for six months, and *just*
*may* close her first sale. "He makes less than he should
to qualify for the loan, but, heck, you have to take a
chance," explained Eunice.

She is not showing any property at this time because
when the sale goes through she plans a trip to Europe on
the proceeds—and wouldn't want to be in the midst of
another "big deal" so that she couldn't get away. When
she returns, she plans to study for her broker's license,
and go into business for herself so that when she makes
another "big deal" she won't have to split the commission with "some joker." If she lists the house and sells it,

too, she reasons she'll get the entire 6 percent—rather than "this measly 1-1/2 percent."

Broker Jim Whitt of Charlottesville, Virginia—in the business for seventeen years—holds a different view.

"The real estate business is a lot like the proverbial iceberg. Most of it isn't visible.

"The obvious part of the business is putting up a 'for sale' sign on a piece of property, then sitting back and waiting for the phone to ring.

"But that's only the beginning. The real work starts once you've found a buyer."

The paper flow, accompanying the sale or purchase of a piece of real estate is something to behold, Realtor Whitt points out. "Bankers, attorneys, the retail merchants association, the buyer, the seller, the agent—a host of people become involved. A typical real estate transaction involves twenty-five or thirty different documents, all of which have to be filled out, approved, shuffled back and forth, and eventually filed. If a government loan is involved—FHA or VA—the number of forms takes another jump.

"To be a top-notch broker," Jim Whitt concludes, "a man or woman has to have the qualities of a good salesperson, a clinical psychologist, a career diplomat, a mortgage banker, a family attorney, and a competent administrator."

### *Before you price photocopying machines, desks, and typewriters.*

After a hard look at your motives to see that they do not resemble Eunice Uninformed's in any recognizable degree, a first step, before you start looking for office space, pricing photocopying machines, desks, and typewriters, and ordering your cards, is some education in small business management. Nothing in the classes taken for your agent's or broker's examination prepares you to operate a business. The National Association of Realtors, through one of its affiliate institutes, offers help if you live near a regional center. Courses are available in business management through most local colleges and universities, and they need not be oriented specifically to real estate, since the problems you will encounter will be largely the same found in any small business.

Be sure that you know the economy of your city or county. Who lives there? Where do they work? How often do they move? Why do they move? Who are your competing brokers and how firmly are they entrenched? How is your area planned and zoned? What changes in the development pattern may be anticipated for the future? What about "Mortgage Market?" How well do you know him? Intimately? Just good friends?? *Never heard of him!*

Three professional people should be consulted before opening a new brokerage: an attorney to draw up necessary papers, an accountant to decide the method of accounting to be used, and an insurance man.

It is impossible, say knowledgeable women, to start a new brokerage on the most stringent scale in most areas of the country for less than $15,000. Starting expenses include such items as office rent and furnishings, supplies, equipment, licenses, stationery and cards, legal fees, accounting fees, insurance policies, artwork, initial advertising, and signs.

The Lewis & Barvin Company of Houston is owned by two sisters, Anne Schultz Lewis and Esther Schultz Barvin. In addition to several years' experience as agents, both held broker's licenses before the firm was opened. Esther for two years, and Anne for six.

"A woman—or man—would be mad to attempt to start up a brokerage without working for someone else for a number of years," said Anne Lewis. "As an agent you find out whether you're in the right business. Obtaining a broker's license gives you added knowledge, and placing it with another broker for a few years gives you an insight into what brokerage entails."

Lewis and Barvin have been in business for four years. They opened with "just the two of us, plus one other agent." There are now six working out of their suburban Houston office.

"It's best to start out with as few agents as possible," Esther said. "Some people seem to think that because you're not paying the agent a salary, he or she doesn't cost you anything. But, each desk costs money. Some high-powered companies estimate that each desk costs $10,000 a year now. It used to be $2,000, then $4,000, $6,000."

"And, advertising is very expensive," Anne interjected. "You can go broke just advertising."

Both sisters confided that they had misgivings about giving up excellent incomes as agents for the uncertain future—but the certain headaches—of brokerage. Neither has regretted it. Both have found brokerage far more stimulating than sales. "And, we need not have worried about giving up our agent's income. We both have higher net incomes now."

"What are some of the 'certain headaches' of real estate brokerage?"

They named two, but assured me that the aches and pains of brokerage were so numerous, you'd swear you were a hypochondriac, if you didn't know better.

"If an agent comes in and says, 'I can't work with this man anymore,' you take over. In other words, you work with the agent's 'rejects,' " said Anne.

"And you work when the need arises—no matter what family plans you've made."

"Because you can't allow expensive advertising to be wasted," Esther explained. "The agent may be able to—but not the broker-owner. Not if she wants to stay in business."

"Does brokerage give you more time overall with your family?"

"Overall—yes," they both agreed.

"What about money?" I asked. "How much should a woman have to open a small office in a large metropolitan area such as this?"

"If she's been successful as an agent," Anne said, "she'll have ample cash to start her own brokerage firm by the time she's gained the experience needed."

"And, if she hasn't been successful as an agent?" Esther asked. "Well, she certainly has no business attempting a brokerage firm!"

Dorothy Martin, president of the franchised Hearthstone Gallery of Homes in Montvale, New Jersey, pointed out some of the aches and pains facing the new broker in an article written for *Real Estate Today*.

"As a successful salesperson with another firm, she probably has had little or no experience managing and administrating. Suddenly she must sell houses, run an effective public relations program, recruit and manage salespeople, and teach neophyte licensees the business.

"Unless the new broker is—or can learn to be—an expert time manager, she may be doomed to a mediocre livelihood," Dorothy said.

Dorothy believes that it is better to begin as a one-person office and very carefully expand.

"A broker's future," she said, "is in the hands of her salespeople whose personalities must match the image the broker wants her office to project."

If you plan to run a dynamic, high-volume office, you will need that type of salesperson. If you are a low-key person whose main objective is to project an image of capable, soft-sell counselors, you will be looking for quite a different person.

## Help from the Small Business Administration.

If, in spite of several successful years as an agent, circumstances (spelled a family to support) preclude your having saved the money to open a brokerage, help may be possible through the Small Business Administration.

Money obtained from the SBA cannot be used to buy or invest in real estate. It can, however, be used for any business expense involved in the selling of real estate. This can include renting or leasing office space or even constructing a building for use exclusively as an office.

There are other restrictions, but even considering them, the majority of real estate offices qualify for initial opening purposes or for expansion.

Your first step is to request a regular business loan from your bank. If you qualify—forget SBA. Your credit is *too* good.

If the bank will not make a loan, ask them to prepare a loan guarantee package for the Small Business Administration. The SBA will investigate your credit and will want to see that you have some collateral to secure the loan. Unlike banks, the SBA does not require 100 percent collateral and will take secondary mortgages on property. If the bank does not want to handle your application through an SBA loan guarantee program (the bank still stands to lose 10 percent), you may apply for a participation or direct loan directly with SBA.

Be sure to allow from two to six months processing time for an SBA loan. For further information on this program, contact any SBA field office. Small Business Administration offices also hold full-day business workshops, detailing factors involved in planning a business, steps necessary to establish a business, and available sources of information, assistance and counsel.

## Franchising. Can you survive without it?

Century 21 International, the nation's fastest growing franchising firm, boasts 5,232 offices in forty-nine states and Canada. A remarkable achievement, considering that the company was formed in 1972. According to Bruce Oseland, director of communications for the firm, the rate of growth is about two hundred offices a month! Gross annual sales, $15 billion!

Century 21 claims that they are giving the local real estate broker a national image—something that didn't exist before. One of their innovations was the pioneering of mass media advertising. This year, the company will spend $15 million on advertising. (Each broker will chip in a mandatory 2 percent of his gross commissions.) But, this is image advertising, and does not include classified and other newspaper advertising that each franchised broker also must run.

In addition, each broker pays 6 percent of his commissions as a franchise fee to the regional master franchiser.

"Can a woman still venture forth and open an office on her own, or must she go with a franchise?" I asked Ida Dirks of Houston.

"It depends on the individual. I would not go with a franchise, though they call on me frequently. And why not? That's their business. They're selling a product.

Their product is franchising. Mine's real estate."

Ida entered Houston real estate as an agent in 1970. Three years later, she passed her broker's examination and opened her first office—with one associate. She now has two offices and twenty-four associates. Her business is mainly residential and she has handled homes from $20,000 to half a million dollars.

"The main advantage of the franchise, I feel, is the referral service," she said. "In our mobile society, every broker must belong to some referral system. There are so many of these systems now that the number of independent brokers who can refer to you is limited."

Kitty Ellis and Nancy Royer, relocation counselor and relocation coordinator, respectively, with Baxter and Swinford, one of Houston's largest multifirms, revealed that approximately one million white-collar managers and executives transfer interstate each year, and forty million people move somewhere in the United States each year. There are now over forty referral services nationwide competing for the transferee. One of the largest, RELO (Inter-City Relocation Service), has approximately nine hundred brokers in nine thousand communities in the United States and overseas; and over twenty thousand sales associates. The referral fee is 10 percent of commission received by a RELO member for selling a client, or commission received for selling a listing referral. Five percent goes to RELO and 5 percent to the referring broker.

Jean Lanphar holds the title of "Business Development Representative" for the internationally franchised Realty World in its Birmingham, Michigan, regional headquarters.

"The day of the independent broker is past," said Jean. "In addition to the usual advantages of franchising, we offer an additional service. A representative visits each of our offices once a month. If the broker is having problems—organizational, managerial, etc., we are there with the professional expertise of a large world-wide organization to help him solve them."

Jean is a licensed broker, and also spent several years as a sales manager. She now works on a salary plus 5 percent commission of the service fee paid to the regional office. She services Realty World offices in four Michigan counties.

"I find this more interesting than general brokerage," she said, "though many women might not agree.

"That's the great thing about this business. Once she gets that license, a woman has many choices as to what she'll do with it—how she'll use it."

The woman determined to go into the brokerage business for herself has several approaches to choose from.

She may open up independent and remain so— limiting herself to a low-key operation, usually up to six sales personnel—as have Anne Barvin and Esther Lewis. "You don't have to be the biggest to have an excellent income. But, you must attempt to be the best," said Esther.

If she wishes to remain independent but expand, a good way of doing so is by adopting the methodology of the real estate chain. Expansion can spread business overhead. "I opened my own firm," said Ida Dirks, "so that I might have more control over my time—more time to spend with my husband and children. I think expansion will eventually make it possible to reach that goal."

If the new broker decides to franchise, she may affiliate with a local, regional, or national organization. Dorothy Martin of Montvale, New Jersey, chose a national organization, Gallery of Homes, the oldest and largest residential real estate brokerage network. "I feel you need a national identity to succeed in this day and age. We still maintain the personal touch with our ads."

Another alternative is broker association, wherein an independent broker gives up her offices and affiliates with other brokers in order to reduce initial capital and continuing overhead costs.

Still another is the "broker cooperative," wherein a well-known trademark or trade name provides the needed market identity; yet, the broker maintains a strong element of individual control over the business, allowing more time to spend on sales.

Whichever plan you choose, industry experts agree that if you have drive and determination, and have acquired the education, experience, and capital needed, your chances for success as a broker are excellent. Women are proving it in every state, every year— proving the words of Dorothy Martin of New Jersey, "This is the greatest business in the world for a woman. A natural!!"

NOTE: Eunice Uninformed, after the shortest real estate career on record, is now into fig newtons and peanut clusters in a large building with several counters in Azusa. She plans a trip to Cucamonga.

# CHAPTER 11

## How to Make $2,000 a Month and Leave Your Car in the Garage

"I have a friend who got her license the same week I got mine. She went into resales with a top company, and I went into on-site selling. Two months later she hadn't sold a thing. I sold five houses the first week after I got my license."

Attractive Gene Rasmussen of Houston, Texas, is an "on-site missionary." And, why not? In her first year in real estate she generated over $4 million in new home sales.

On-site, or subdivision selling, was once looked upon as a real estate kindergarten by the establishment (spelled men), where greenhorns (spelled women) could undergo fiery baptismals without causing the collapse of the industry. It was hoped.

No more. Scenes such as the ones described below have made on-site selling of choice developments eagerly sought-after plums.

It was barely dawn in Orange County, California, when the first car pulled into a flag-marked parking lot.

The occupants, a man and a woman, adjusted their bodies to more relaxed positions, and opened a thermos of coffee. The parking lot began to fill around them. By 9:30 approximately three thousand families were poised for what one man described as the "Great Orange County Home Rush." The scene was "Woodbridge" and the occupants of Buicks, Mercedes, Volks, Cadillacs, and Fords were there to compete for 221 homes priced from $50,000 to $100,000. Selection of buyers would be by lottery!

At an appointed hour, electric trams went into operation to ferry the crowds to the "gaming area." The lower priced homes—$50,000 to $60,000—drew the largest crowd. A man's name was called near the back of the crowd and he made his way forward.

"My God," said an amazed observer, "it's like winning a door prize at a lawn party. Your name is called and you get a thirty-year mortgage!"

As the winner of the thirty-year mortgage moved through the crowd, hands reached for his sleeve.

"I'll give you two thousand profit."

"I'll make it four."

"Five."

"Hell. I'll make it ten."

Most of the participants in the lottery were buying as an investment. They planned to rent the home out for six months to a year, then sell. The anticipated profit? From $25,000 to $30,000!

A few miles distant, one of Southern California's largest home lotteries was held on a Saturday afternoon. Names were drawn for the chance to buy 282 residences. Prices for 55 of the homes were the highest ever asked in Rossmoor Corporation's Leisure World—$99,000 to $127,000. Elm Weingarden, vice-president of corporate marketing, revealed that many customers had waited months to buy one of the homes, and that the lottery method was conceived as "the fairest method" for purchasers. "Speculators are not welcome," said Mr. Weingarden. "All purchasers will be asked to sign a pledge that they will live in the homes."

Another Southern California firm, Larwin, set an all-time one-week company sales record—34 homes valued at $2.8 million. "We've been in business since 1948, and this is a record for the company in both number of homes sold at one community and total dollar volume," Monty Polson, the firm's vice-president and director of marketing, said.

In Sacramento's Campus Commons development, customers arrived with camp cots, sleeping bags, and chairs to purchase homes that would not be completed for approximately four months and would not be placed on the market for thirty-six hours. Did would-be purchasers maintain a thirty-six-hour vigil, suffer the indignity of rolling out sleeping bags, subsisting on thermos coffee and sandwiches, and sitting up all night in canvas chairs in order to take advantage of subsidized government housing—five bedrooms, two baths, and an extra pair of pants for $16,500? No, the homes were priced from the mid-fifties to the high-sixties with conventional financing. When the sales office opened, the units were snapped up within minutes. "Have-nots" were offering "haves" on-the-spot profit for their commitment. There were no takers. As in Southern California, a good number of the "players" were buying for investment purposes.

While not every woman engaged in on-site selling has clients dropping at her feet to clutch her skirt while beseeching her to sell them a home, many women find subdivision, or on-site sales, a lucrative area of the real estate business and much prefer it to resales. The key to on-site success lies in the quality of your product.

## $2,800 a month in Houston.

"If you have a quality product to sell in a proven area of town, you can make it big," said wife, mother, and on-site saleswoman Gene Rasmussen.

Prior to becoming Girl Friday four years ago in Houston's master-planned community, Oak Creek Village, Gene had never worked. With her husband in Korea and her three children in school all day, she wanted "something interesting to do." She took what has proven to be a wise first step—an office job in the development she now sells. "I became familiar with the subdivision and the builders," she said, "and the sales manager encouraged me to go into sales."

In her first year, she generated over $4 million in new home sales.

I asked her about the objection to on-site selling voiced by some women. "Do you find it confining?"

"Not at all. I put in five days a week here in the office—nine to five. But my hours are very flexible. If I need time for something personal, I work it out with one of the salesmen."

On-site selling, Gene pointed out, eliminates the pressure to obtain listings. You deal only with the people who come in to look at your homes. You're selling new merchandise at a fixed price. There are no offers at nine P.M. to be delivered across town before you can go to bed that night. No counteroffers as you're sitting down to dinner.

"The newcomer to real estate," she said, "is likely to get her first check sooner in on-site sales than in general real estate—usually two months sooner. In resales, you might go three or four months before you make your first sale, then it'd be another two months before your commission check came through.

"The volume of prospects is so much greater, it stands to reason you're going to make your first sale sooner. Not all the people who come through are good prospects, of course, but the experience of talking to these people—polishing your presentation—is invaluable."

Subdivision selling offers the extra advantage of using diversions (not to be confused with adjusting your bra strap or launching into a description of the movie you saw on the late show—complete with dialogue). Rather; What changes would Mr. and Mrs. Prospect like to make in the house—as owners? What colors would they prefer in the kitchen? Yellow? White is always good, works with everything. And, the baths? Do they like wallpaper? If the conversation can be guided in this direction, the chances are good that the sales will be made.

Subdivision, or on-site selling, also offers sales personnel the use of the narrative technique. You have full knowledge of who has bought; how many children there are in the area; what ages, etc. This is a distinct advantage, as most clients want to get the feel of a community before committing themselves to purchase.

"What about commissions? Aren't they lower?" I asked Gene Rasmussen.

"On the contrary. We get 2 percent of the sale price of the home. Our homes sell for $50,000 to $98,000. That's a better commission than the new agent is going to make in general real estate. Unless you're both lister and seller, your commission is going to be 1-1/2 percent of the total of that 6 percent commission.

"I sell two of these homes a month, on an annual average. Maybe none, in some of the winter months—but two or three sometimes in July or August."

Using $70,000 as an average figure, I estimated Gene's income at $2,800 a month.

Women doing on-site selling in lower priced developments should do as well as in the medium or higher priced areas, Gene said. "In some FHA and GI developments, the agent might make only $500 a sale, but her volume of sales would be so much greater than here, in an area where the average price is $70,000, it works out about the same. These incomes are, of course, contingent on having a good product to sell."

"How do you define a 'good product'?"

"If the location is wrong, the homes are impractical or shoddily built, and the builder is uncooperative, you can put in your time—nine to five—forever, without making a sale.

"Anything that certain builders put up is going to be a winner. A good builder works with the salespeople. He wants to know if anyone is asking for Colonials? 'What do the customers think of the dining room closed off?' he asks. 'Would they rather have it open?' 'What do they think of the half-bath in the laundry room?' 'Would they rather have it as a powder room off the entrance hall?' "

In deciding whether to become affiliated with a development, Gene Rasmussen believes the saleswoman should study the track record of the builder involved. Does he build a solid home? Does he go back to service his homes cheerfully if there are bugs to be ironed out?

"If a builder gets a bad reputation—leaking pipes that are not fixed, floors that sag—word gets around," she said. "Sometimes word of mouth. Sometimes there are so many complaints it's picked up by the papers.

"Never," she emphasized, "become involved with a poor builder. I've seen women 'turned-off' on on-site selling because they were trying to sell an impossible product. If you're a newcomer, find out something about the builder or builders you'll be working with. Be selective. Proceed cautiously. There are knowledgeable women in this area of real estate who simply take a vacation if there is not a project opening up that they think will sell well. And, why not? Why put in your time trying to sell someone's mistake?"

## $40,000 a year in San Diego.

There were systems of condominium ownership in various parts of Europe as far back as the twelfth century. One authority has traced the condominium back to the ancient Hebrews. But this method of ownership apparently caused so many problems that, by the middle of the nineteenth century, European legislation either did not provide for systems of apartment ownership or specifically prohibited them. In America, condominiums made their debut at the instigation of the Federal Housing Administration in the early sixties. Today condominium projects are a major factor in the real estate industry, from the modestly priced Century Village East at Deerfield Beach, Florida, where units run from $16,900 to $35,000, to San Diego's Coronado Shores, where the retired school teacher or grocery clerk may purchase a four-bedroom and den corner condo with both ocean and bay view for $375,000, to New York's Olympia Tower at Fifth Avenue and 51st Street, where the last of six penthouses sold for $650,000.

In the late sixties, while many builders continued to level sites for traditional tract homes, others sensed a vacuum. Following the example of European communities, enterprising builders determined to build condominiums for upper- and middle-income families, primarily the "empty nesters." They offered the same amenities found in private homes in a similar price range—rooms large enough to accommodate any type or size furnishings, fireplaces, dressing rooms, laundry rooms, an abundance of closet and storage space, private patios and garden areas, double garages with automatic door-openers—with the added attraction of spacious common areas—including clubhouses, swimming pools, and tennis courts. A monthly fee covered use of the facilities and assured maintenance of home exteriors and common areas.

The sale of this type condominium has proved a particularly lucrative field for real estate women. Mary Floyd of San Diego has been selling condominium projects for the past ten years, with an income of between $30,000 and $40,000 a year.

"I was widowed ten years ago, when my children were sixteen and eleven years old," she said. "People asked, 'How can you take a job that does not assure a steady income when you have children to support?'

"It's true that women in this business can't be sure of an exact amount, but if you're doing your job right—your income is assured. And it's an income higher than any salary available to a middle-aged widow entering the labor force!" she added.

Five years ago Mary became sales representative for Coronado Shores, a resort condominium project stretching along the Pacific Ocean, with 1,500 units in ten separate buildings. Two-bedroom condominiums were priced from $85,000 to $125,000; two bedrooms plus den for $155,000 to $325,000; and four bedrooms plus den for $375,000—without den, $350,000.

Mary's commission on sales varies, 1 percent on some, she said, 1-1/2 percent on others, and 2 percent on still others.

I asked if the 1 percent commission applied to the higher priced units—$350,000, $375,000?

"No, the higher commission rate is paid on the 'slow movers'—no matter what the price."

Mary Floyd, like Gene Rasmussen of Houston, lives in the development she's selling.

"Who buys luxury condominiums—besides real estate women?"

"People who want the freedom to travel. People who are tired of digging in the garden, running the mower—or finding someone to run the mower for them, and never knowing whether they'll show up. People who like the idea of a twenty-four-hour security guard, well-maintained tennis courts, pools, clubhouses, saunas.

"We have many singles living here—widows and widowers; divorced men and women; young, unmarried businessmen aware that it's to their advantage tax-wise to buy, rather than rent. We also have a few foreign buyers. A Mexican family. A German family."

"No Arab oil sheiks?"

"No sheiks."

Mary feels that on-site selling offers a woman a more dignified way of real estate life than general residential real estate. "You meet prospects in an office," she said, "explain the layout, prices, amenities, etc.—and show the models. If they're interested, you take them out to see the construction and the exact location of their future unit. There is no need to leave the grounds of your development." Like Gene Rasmussen of Houston, Mary did not care for regular resale work. "I hate to drive, make pleasant conversation, and find addresses all at the same time."

She finished with, "I believe that on-site selling gives a woman an excellent income, and affords her more time with her family. And that's what we all strive for."

Another way of saying, "Any woman who has a career and a family develops something in the way of two personalities. Her problem is to keep one from draining the life from the other."

# CHAPTER 12

## How to Use
## Your Real Estate License
## for a Salaried Job

*Respectable means rich, and decent*
*means poor. I should die if I heard*
*my family called decent.*
Thomas Peacock,
Crocket's Castle

*The sales manager.*

Once upon a time (yesterday morning, in some benighted offices), the novice female agent, her apron strings barely untied, and her license so new it squeaked, was shown a desk, introduced to any agents who just happened to be present at that particular moment, patted on the back or thigh by her male coach and exhorted to "go out there and sell like a man, honey."

"Training in my first office," said a successful veteran of fifteen years, "consisted of being led to a desk I was to share with another agent and presented with a bill for $40.00 for enough calling cards to 'call' on every damn house in town and some wooden FOR SALE signs on stakes, carrying my name and phone number underneath the firm's.

"I had read that you could 'live on your listings,' and the idea of sitting back and snipping listing coupons, while you watched your favorite soap opera sounded pretty good.

" 'How do you get listings, so you can live on your listings?' I asked the male at the next desk.

" 'Go out and ring doorbells,' he said.

" 'And then?'

" 'Ask them if they want to list their house,' he barked.

"I held my first open house 'cold'—wrote out my first deposit receipt with my hand shaking so badly my clients probably thought I had an advanced case of palsy.

"I made enough money that year to pay for my gas and the damned signs and cards."

In today's highly competitive field, the sales manager's training program includes instruction for new agents in a myriad of duties—all calculated to spell SUCCESS for agent and company. How to take floor time. How to write an ad. Assembling comparables. Using sources of information (MLS books, tax office records, cross-reference telephone directories, tax maps, etc.). Taking listings. Finding prospects. Showing a house. Qualifying. Writing an offer. Methods of financing. Data on property taxes and income tax consequences pertaining to a sale. Estimating closing costs. Escrow procedures. Building a referral system.

A sales manager may earn from $1,000 a month to $6,000, or $7,000, depending on company, manager, and plan of remuneration. Incomes are based on one of three plans: (1) straight salary, (2) salary plus an override based on the staff's or company's production, and (3) either of the above combined with the manager's own commissions earned from listings and sales. An override with a guaranteed minimum is sometimes used, as is the further incentive of bonus-type remuneration, based on gross or net profit levels. The growing number of women wearing the distinguished mantle of sales manager has served to bury the myth that leadership ability is essentially a male quality.

Are you a likely candidate for this lucrative, highly prestigious area of the profession?

The one essential quality for management is, of course, leadership ability. Since it is a quality more difficult to define than to perceive, listed below are some questions designed to help you in your decision.

Are you an establisher of morale, rather than a reactor to morale?

An instigator, rather than a perpetrator?

A puncher, rather than a counterpuncher?

Do you possess that ingredient of personality which causes others to follow you?

Are you a problem solver?

Able to enlighten and exhort?

Capable of accomplishment through other people?

Are you a good administrator—confident of your ability to run the show?

A recommended first step toward a career in management is a broker's license to hang alongside your agent's license. This gives you not only the knowledge necessary to perform your job well, but the authority to train and lead.

Your personal training program—like the training program you will set up for your agents—should be ongoing. It will include attending educational meetings and seminars offered through the National Association. Ideas abound for education in management in books, tapes, and films that may be purchased or rented. Classes pertaining to motivation, communication, business management, and related topics are offered through local universities and private schools. Managers who do not take advantage of opportunities to learn new techniques, changing market situations, changing tax and finance regulations, may find themselves in the unenviable position of being less knowledgeable than the men and women they are directing (attempting to direct?).

THE MANAGER'S CONTRACT.

Your contract should always be in writing. No reputable firm makes the rules as they go along. And before signing a contract with a company you should inform yourself on the reputation and stability of the company, its affiliations, referral system, etc.

Donna Jo King is owner-president of a Colorado firm (Weidman & Co.) with twelve branch offices. She is also a director of the National Association of Realtors on the national as well as state level. She employs a sales manager for each company office and enters into a three-page contract with her managers.

"All of my managers are brokers," she said.

"How are they compensated?

"By salary plus an override based on office production."

Her manager-brokers also list and sell, she said. "They start out with a sixty-forty split on their personal production rather than the fifty-fifty split that the salespeople receive."

One of the first conditions of the contract is the requirement that the manager read and be governed by the Code of Ethics of the National Association of Realtors, the real estate law for the State of Colorado, and the by-laws of the local real estate board.

The obligations of both manager and company are set forth, and the duties of the manager are outlined in detail.

INTERVIEWING AND HIRING.

In her organizational role, the manager's most important task is that of acquiring and training salespeople.

The type of information given by the prospective recruit will be determined by the techniques used by the sales manager in the initial interview.

Listed below are five musts on interviewing:

1. Have applicants fill out an application form giving data about family, education, experience, and health before you begin the interview. The form should also ask for character references. Let your prospects have time to look over the information beforehand—don't "throw" the questionnaires at them.

2. Know where you are going when you start the interview. If you don't, you're likely to lose yourself and the interviewee. "I didn't know what the hell the woman wanted to know," said one outraged male agent after an interview with a female sales manager (now back pounding a beat).

3. Present all facts and figures honestly in order to eliminate later disputes and misconceptions.

4. Become a master of the art of asking leading questions so that you may assess ego-drive, motivation, ability to work consistently, and how well the prospective new agent gets along with people.

THE AGENT'S CONTRACT.

The contract which the manager offers the new agent should spell out all rights and obligations of both parties. Carrying this procedure further, Donna King has a policy and procedure manual posted in each of her twelve offices, tailored to the particular needs of her company.

The company has a four-level training course which includes basic orientation, O.J.T. sessions, sales training, and continuing education through local colleges and universities.

All sales, Donna said, are closed by the broker-manager of the office involved. "The salesperson is encouraged to attend, but the manager has the responsibility of seeing that the myriad details and legalities are taken care of."

In addition to her duties as a director of the National Association, Donna is also state chairman for Make America Beautiful, the public relations arm of the National Association. She lives on a Colorado cattle ranch—"We're third generation on the ranch"—with her husband and two children and commutes twenty-five miles each day to her corporate headquarters. I talked to her on a busy Saturday morning. "What do you do on Sunday?" I asked the soft-spoken young executive.

"Teach Sunday school."

Is there a formula for success in sales management? "No," said blonde Loretta Sokol, sales manager for Marston Real Estate, a large Alaska firm.

"You have to know your territory. Some of the policies I advocate in Alaska might not prove effective in other areas.

"In Alaska, a home is part of a woman's mental health, because she spends so much time in it. With the days short in winter, and long in summer, it's doubly important that children have friends, so we don't isolate a mother with young children. And our properties must have a place for hockey equipment, ski equipment, sleds, heavy clothing, snowmobiles. We don't push a home that doesn't meet those requirements."

The mother of two grade school children, Loretta had sold houses for her company only one and one-half years when she was asked to help train new agents. She works on a salary plus a percentage of the company dollar, and has twenty-four agents, twelve men and twelve women working under her.

"Interestingly enough," she said, "the most successful agent in residential sales is a male, and the top commercial agent is a woman."

How does the cliche, "Alaska is not a place to live, but a way of life," apply to real estate, I asked.

"You'd think," she said, "that in a country with subzero weather, where property is sometimes shown by snowmobile, four-wheel-drive vehicles, and planes, that door-to-door canvassing would be the last method employed by agents to obtain listings, but some agents find this method quite lucrative—especially in the worst winter months.

"Who," she asked with a smile, "is going to let a woman stand on the doorstep in subzero weather, or slam the door in her face with the snow swirling around her?"

She pointed this out as another example of "knowing your territory"—regardless of the formal ongoing training the manager receives.

"January is generally considered a poor month in the Lower Forty-eight," she continued, "but in Alaska it's sometimes our best month. Cabin fever sets in. Looking at new homes is one way to bring the fever down."

AGENTS DO NOT LEARN BY THEIR MISTAKES.

A sales manager is a trainer, a problem-solver, and a motivator. She has an eye for efficient business methods. She has a sixth sense that tells her when a salesman or saleswoman, successful in another area, has selected real estate for the wrong reason—"The money's better."

She avoids the personal tragedy which accompanies failure by proceeding very slowly when hiring new people—and cautions her prospects to take the same attitude when deciding on real estate as a profession, and selecting a company.

She does not embrace the philosophy that agents learn by their mistakes!

## Appraising.

"We just walked through the ice and snow and went over the Baltic Sea to the Island of Sylt in the North Sea. Later, I joined relatives who were also refugees in Cologne." Irmgard Patterson described her flight from the Russian army as it approached East Prussia in 1945.

In Cologne, without finishing high school, she did a secretary apprenticeship "for very little pay." In 1955, she left Germany, came to America, and became secretary to a real estate appraiser in Chicago.

Today, Irmgard is one of fifteen women nationally to be admitted to the prestigious, professionally exacting American Institute of Real Estate Appraisers. Headquartered in Honolulu, business takes her to Guam, Fiji, Taiwan, Saipan, Yap, and Palau.

Her clients include banks, loan companies, and developers. Her job is a mixture of real estate valuation and counseling; and her assignments include studies of highest and best use, development and redevelopment of income properties, resort-oriented projects, shopping centers, industrial properties, hotels, and office buildings.

She also does analyses in conjunction with architectural and planning firms for master-planned communities and public improvements.

"For hotels, you've got to really watch what the tourist industry is doing. For offices, check the occupancy potential," she said.

"First, you inspect the property; then study floor plans, building plans, construction cost data and development costs. Check on the value of the land. To estimate it, see what other similar properties have been marketed for in the neighborhood.

"Then you check how much income it would generate and total the expense: construction, operating costs, ground rent, taxes, and a reserve fund for replacements."

Real estate appraising, a little known but lucrative career, is open to all—men, women, young, mature, minorities and handicapped. Earnings vary. Starting salaries for Government Housing Authority appraisers fall just below $17,000 a year. A recent opening at the federal Housing and Urban Development Department paid $37,000 a year. Experienced real estate fee appraisers can earn anywhere from $30,000 a year to $100,000 a year, depending on complexity of assignments and type of properties—moderate-priced single dwellings or multimillion-dollar developmental projects.

Education in appraising is offered through regular enrollment or extension division courses in colleges and universities, and through the education departments of the American Institute of Real Estate Appraisers, the Society of Real Estate Appraisers, and the National Association of Independent Fee Appraisers.

A sampling of the courses offered by the American Institute of Real Estate Appraisers includes; basic principles, methods and techniques, capitalization theory and techniques, urban properties, rural properties, condemnation, investment analysis, industrial properties, single-family residential appraisal, and appraisal administration.

If you are a young woman contemplating a career in real estate appraising, a real estate degree from a college or university will give you a "head start." Some studies in computer technology would also be helpful, since computer use has revolutionized the appraising profession.

If you are a not-so-young woman, the fact that most appraisers come from the ranks of real estate brokers and agents should be encouraging. A background of market knowledge acquired through selling real estate is helpful in making judgment decisions, say men and women who have entered the field through real estate sales. Many come into appraising through the related areas of mortgage lending, title, and escrow.

GENERAL DEFINITIONS OF APPRAISING.

The appraisal of real estate is the art of assembling and analyzing facts relating to the solution of a problem concerning valuation or evaluation of property and forming a conclusion with respect to such problem.

Valuation of real estate is defined as an estimate of the market value of a particular property or interest therein, at a given time.

Evaluation of real estate pertains to studies of the nature, quality or utility of a property or any interest in or aspect of real property, which provide solutions to real estate problems but do not necessarily include an estimate of market value. Such studies include land utilization, economic feasibility, highest and best use of a particular property, and marketability or investment quality of a particular proposed or existing property.

A real estate appraisal report is the means by which an

appraisal is transmitted to a client or a third party. The report may be written or oral.

A narrative real estate appraisal report is a report that not only sets forth the opinion or conclusion of the appraiser with respect to the solution of a problem concerning the valuation or evaluation of real estate, but also contains (1) a reasonably complete statement of the relevant factual data assembled in the course of the appraisal process; (2) a reasonably complete statement of the appraiser's analysis of the relevant factual data; and (3) a reasonably complete statement of the reasoning supporting the appraiser's opinion or conclusion. If the report itself does not set forth all of the above, the file of the appraiser must contain a reasonably complete memorandum thereof.

A form real estate appraisal report is a real estate appraisal reported in or upon a form which permits the appraiser to summarize both the conclusion and the relevant factual data assembled in the course of the appraisal process.

In order to qualify for the complex assignments in real estate appraising commanding the more lucrative fees, membership in a nationally recognized professional appraisal organization is mandatory.

The American Institute of Real Estate Appraisers (430 North Michigan Avenue, Chicago, Illinois 60611), an affiliate of the National Association of Realtors, was founded in 1932. It offers two professional designations: (1) Resident Member (must have passed the Institute examination and have five years' experience in real estate, including two years of appraising), and (2) Member Appraisal Institute (must have passed highly specialized examinations and have five years of appraisal experience).

The Society of Real Estate Appraisers (7 South Dearborn Street, Chicago, Illinois 60603), the largest independent association of professional real estate appraisers and analysts in North America, was founded in 1935. There are 186 chapters throughout the United States, Canada, and the Caribbean, and over eighteen thousand members. The society offers three professional designations: (1) Senior Residential Appraiser (trained and experienced in the appraisal of residential properties), (2) Senior Real Property Appraiser (must pass certain courses, have eight years' experience appraising income producing properties, experience in the preparation of real estate market studies and feasibility analysis reports), and (3) Senior Real Estate Analyst (trained and experienced in the appraisal and analysis of all types of real estate interests and ownerships and qualified to extend the appraisal analysis beyond current market value to provide a basis for decision-making to clients). The SREA designation is awarded for five years only. To be recertified, an SREA must submit evidence of continued professional training and performance.

Detailed information on each organization and its requirements may be obtained by writing to the addresses listed.

Generally, membership in a professional appraiser organization offers such benefits as active contact with federal agencies using the services of real estate appraisers, counseling on state government activities, regional conferences, services of a Market Data Center (a network of regional centers designed to process and publish current market data on a national basis for lending institutions and qualified independent fee appraisers), professional journals, weekly newsletters, a Directory of Government Appraisal Officers, appraisal guides, educational courses, seminars, and workshops.

If the possibility of overcoming such seemingly insurmountable obstacles as economic feasibility, relevant factual data, capitalization, cost of replacement, and cost analysis for master-planned communities seems as remote as the possibility that you will write your next deposit receipt standing on your head on the kitchen drainboard of a "three bedroom, two bath"— with your hair and skirt covering your face—take heart.

"ANY WOMAN WHO CAN MEASURE OUT A DRESS
CAN MEASURE OUT A HOUSE."
    The words are VA appraiser Kay Murray's.
    Orphaned at thirteen, and raised by relatives in one of Los Angeles's black ghetto neighborhoods, soft-voiced, charming Kay Murray is living proof of what the real estate profession has to offer women. A broker for thirty years, and an appraiser for ten, she also holds a Class B-1 California Contractor's license.
    "I've worked since I was thirteen years old, doing any odd jobs I could get in the neighborhood while I was in school. Having to go to work at thirteen gave me a head start. I learned real young that the women in the neighborhood who were making the best money were in real estate."
    "Would you encourage women to pursue a career in appraising?"
    "Definitely," she said. "It's a field they can come into at any age, and there isn't the competition or pressure you find in sales.
    "Some women with children to support must have that paycheck at the end of the week or month. They can't take a chance on making those big commissions.
    "There are presently so few women in appraising," said Kay, "that when I call an office for information, they automatically assume I'm calling for my boss. They

don't even consider the possibility that I'm the appraiser—that the information is for my own use."

Kay obtained her formal education in appraising through the University of California Extension Division courses, she told me. "What are the job prospects for a woman once she completes her training?" I asked.

"I've talked to some women who tell me that it's the same story in appraising as in other fields—'How much experience have you had?' 'They won't hire me as a fee appraiser unless I've had experience,' they say. 'But how do I get experience?'

"I advise them to get on with a lending institution. They can come in at a salary of $700 or $800 a month, plus a car or mileage. When they've advanced to the point—experience and education-wise—to qualify for the more complex assignments, they may elect to stay with the company, become an independent fee appraiser, or go with their state government or the federal government, in one of the higher paid positions open to more experienced appraisers."

RURAL APPRAISING.

Modern-day history records several instances of fearless women entering the posted, "ENTER AT YOUR OWN RISK," male encampment of rural appraising. In each recorded instance, the women have returned unscathed—makeup intact, skirt straight, no buttons missing on blouse. The only complaints heard had to do with the condition of the fearless ladies' shoes.

There are four types of rural appraisals: (1) appraisal for a farm lending agency, (2) appraisal for market value, (3) appraisal for tax assessing agencies, and (4) appraisal for eminent domain.

The general physical and economic factors to be considered in rural appraising include climatic conditions, soils, topography, buildings, type of farming, markets, past and present prices for crops produced, leasing information and characteristics of local land market. Special appraisal procedures applying to rural appraising include irrigation and drainage, ranch appraisal, leasehold, and personal property.

Membership in the American Society of Farm Managers and Rural Appraisers (P. O. Box 6857, Denver, Colorado 80206), a professional organization devoted to the management of farms and the appraisal of rural real estate, is open to women able to meet academic and experience requirements of the society. Founded in 1929, it now has approximately one thousand eight hundred members, most of them located in the United States.

The society provides meetings where rural appraisers may learn from recognized authorities and each other; conducts training schools in rural and ranch appraisals; administers an accreditation program for its members; cooperates with and supports agencies striving to improve American agriculture. It is also responsible for the publication of a professional journal.

If the possibility of making a market-value appraisal for a Kansas grain farm, an eminent domain appraisal for a New Jersey dairy farm, a narrative appraisal for an Arizona irrigated farm, a timber appraisal for a Georgia estate, a tax appraisal for a Texas livestock farm, or even a stock ranch appraisal for a Colorado ranch, seems as remote as the possibility of milking a New Jersey cow with one hand while you write a deposit receipt with the other—hang in there! Annette Jones is appraising in Virginia, Nellie Robbins in Indiana, Laurie Jablin in Georgia, Edna Martin and Robi Francisco in California.

## *Property management.*

Our country is still very young—compared to most civilized areas of the world. Not too many years have passed since land now teeming with dwellings, shopping centers, office complexes, industrial parks, and golf courses lay unclaimed. In some instances, the ownership of property today is in the same hands taking original title.

As societies and countries mature, there is an inescapable trend toward the accumulation of large holdings in a relatively few hands. The accumulating of America is proceeding on schedule. Insurance companies, trusts, and institutions of all types (foreign as well as domestic) are picking, gathering, discarding culls from Maine to California—on to Alaska and Hawaii. The demand for competent investment property management is accelerating at a rapid pace, as are opportunities for women, of all ages, in this area of real estate.

WHAT DOES PROPERTY MANAGEMENT ENTAIL?

According to CPM Lillian Bowen of Washington, D.C., it can entail a 12:30 A.M. Sunday call that "A" building has a large leak in a waterpipe on the seventh floor; that several hundred gallons of water were released before the control valve could be closed. A call from the harried resident manager of "B" building: "None of the porters reported for work today, and I don't know what to do with this mountain of trash!" A registered letter—"You are hereby notified to appear," signed, National Labor Relations Board. A telegram from the Department of Human Relations—"A discrimination complaint has been filed. Appear tomorrow and bring all of your records." A letter from Washington

Metropolitan Area Transit—"You are hereby advised that we must excavate below the foundation of Apartment Building 'X' and shore up beneath building." A telephone call from the firm's attorney—"Your L & T case comes up at 10 A.M. I will need you in court." An early morning check of Office Building "G" to ascertain whether the painters showed up. "Gad! They're painting the wrong room!"

Lillian is president of Herbert Harvey, Inc., a large D.C. firm leasing and managing office buildings, apartment buildings, and other commercial structures. She has been associated with the corporation since 1941, and was the first female CPM (Certified Property Manager) in the metropolitan Washington area.

"I have been involved in the management of real estate since I was seven years old," said Lillian. "My grandfather owned several small row houses in our neighborhood and I was assigned to collect the rent every Saturday. The houses were modest and the tenants frequently could not pay. One Saturday, a tenant who had no rent money offered me two white mice instead. I was delighted to accept them. I smuggled them into my mother's dresser drawer, and the next day discovered a family of five. This was my first lesson in real estate: Never make a side deal with a tenant!"

In addition to the details noted by Lillian Bowen, a property management firm interviews and hires resident managers; supervises administrative and maintenance services; prepares project rental leases; arranges for security guard services; coordinates advertising of rentals; rents units and collects rent; handles claims and correspondence, and prepares a management survey.

The property manager also prepares repair and upgrading specifications, solicits bids for same, and awards contracts. Monthly reports are submitted showing collections, disbursements, and comparison of actual expenditures with budgeted amounts. When reserves are accumulated to meet future requirements, the property manager advises and recommends to the board the most appropriate types of secured investments to be found in order to generate as much interest as possible from the reserves.

In addition to the above duties, the management agent must keep informed of changes in municipal codes, state laws, federal laws, and any other applicable regulations.

In effect, the property manager is business manager, friend, counselor, and financial adviser.

BREAKING INTO THE FIELD.

"How does one become a property manager?" I asked Penny Zarecky, director of public rèlations for a California firm with between two and three thousand units nestling under its competent wings.

"The first step is a real estate license, of course.

"Some women go to real estate school with this area in mind—rather than sales. The idea of a salary appeals to them."

"What *about* salaries?"

"That would depend on the applicant's qualifications. Does she have a degree in real estate? Her broker's license? Has she had several years' experience in property management—or a related area?

"The inexperienced, new licensee," she continued, "usually comes in at a salary of $700 or $800 a month—depending on the firm. But, competent property managers move up fast. Most companies have an insurance program as an added incentive, and some allow their managers to purchase stock in the company."

"Suppose a woman wants to start her own firm after she gains some experience?"

"She must have her broker's license in order to head her own firm."

"Are there many doing this?"

"Very few. In fact, there are very few women in property management, and that's a shame—because this is a woman-oriented business. Many of our best people come from the ranks of resident managers. We encourage competent resident managers to go to real estate school, get their license and move up to property management. We also encourage them to obtain the Certified Property Manager designation."

Organized for the benefit of individuals in the management profession, the Institute of Real Estate Management (430 North Michigan Boulevard, Chicago, Illinois 60611), an affiliate of the National Association of Realtors, awards the Certified Property Manager designation. Courses available to candidates for the CPM designation cover management of residential property, office buildings, commercial buildings and shopping centers; managing real estate as an investment; preparing the long-range management plan for residential properties—for office buildings, commercial stores, and shopping centers; the management of condominiums; the workout of troubled HUD properties; and managing the management office. In order to be certified as a CPM, you must meet academic and experience requirements. Currently, Certified Property Managers are responsible for over $70 billion in real property assets in this country and Canada.

Certified Property Managers may apply for accreditation for their management organizations. In order to qualify for the AMO (Accredited Management Organization), firms must prove themselves in compliance with standards established by the Institute of Real Estate Management, including organizational stability, management portfolio, fiscal and operational reliability and education.

The Institute of Real Estate Management also offers a training program for resident managers. The skills taught in the program help deal with the problems encountered daily by working resident managers.

OPPORTUNITIES IN GOVERNMENT HOUSING MANAGEMENT.

"WANTED: Woman to manage 4,000 apartment units in the City and County of Sacramento. Must have experience, expertise, charm, integrity, and a great sense of humor."

The ad never made it to the classified; nevertheless, Carole Tregellas is responsible for the management and maintenance of four thousand housing authority rental units. She controls the annual budget for her department and oversees the work of approximately ninety persons, including assistant managers, clerks and maintenance crews.

"We're responsible for fixing everything from a clogged toilet to a leaky faucet to a torn screen," she said. "We maintain all units—conventional, elderly, and high-rise housing."

Carole has seen public housing grow from zero to four thousand units in her city in less than twenty-five years.

The federal government has become the owner of a number of multifamily properties acquired through the U.S. Department of Housing and Urban Development—projects acquired because of the mortgager's failure to meet financial obligations. HUD's Office of Property Disposition, under the Assistant Secretary for Housing Management, is responsible for the management, reconditioning and sale of the properties, and regularly contracts with private real estate brokers to manage and operate such multifamily properties.

Brokers interested in managing and operating HUD acquired properties are invited to bid on management contracts in their geographic areas.

Daisy Donovan, president of Daisy L. Donovan Real Estate, Inc., of Detroit, is an authority in the area of government housing. Married to a minister, and describing her nationality as "Afro-American," she was the first woman president of the Detroit Real Estate Broker's Association in its forty-seven-year history. She has served as an area management broker, as housing consultant to the City of Detroit, and housing commissioner for the city.

The day I interviewed her, she had just returned from a meeting of the Housing Commission.

"Why do you think so many government-owned properties go into default?" I asked.

After naming poor management as the prime suspect, and pinpointing such areas as lack of preventive maintenance, delinquencies, excessive expenses, and poor resident management personnel, she said bluntly, "Sometimes I think some of these HUD programs were designed for default. Too many of them are not set up right. Not enough money was built in."

The Department of Housing and Urban Development apparently agrees with Mrs. Donovan's frank assessment—though tardily—and is taking steps to alleviate the situation. Early last year, the department awarded grants totaling $660,000 to five universities for the development of academic programs in housing management: Howard University, Washington, D.C.; Southern University, Baton Rouge, Louisiana; Temple University, Philadelphia, Pennsylvania; Texas Southern University, Houston, Texas; and Winston-Salem

State University in Winston-Salem, North Carolina.

The participating schools will develop a training program geared to their own geographical areas and clientele. Programs will incorporate basic housing management performance standards already developed by HUD into a training program that will lead to the certification of qualified managers for HUD-assisted housing.

These programs and courses of study will become a part of the various schools' regular curricula and lead to the development of major fields of study in housing management, or to minor fields such as business administration, urban planning, or social work. In addition, there will be a variety of short-term workshops, institutes and extension courses for people who want and need more training, but are unable to devote full-time to pursuing a general university education.

Each of the five universities will use one or more nearby housing projects as working labs, and will work closely with local housing management personnel—both public and private.

This program should offer further opportunities to women interested in property management. Government openings are now available for qualified urban interns at beginning salaries of approximately $9,000 per year for the first year, with the opportunity to advance to between $10,000 and $11,000 after one year—and in approximately four to five years, $17,000 or above. For information on job opportunities and various training programs, contact the administrative officer in your local HUD office.

AN EIGHTEEN-HOUR DAY, OR AN EIGHTEEN-HOUR WEEK?
THE CHOICE IS YOURS.

Petite young Casey Blackwell of Tucson, Arizona,

sometimes works an eighteen-hour day. "And I wear six or seven hats," she said.

Casey moved to Tucson after eight years in real estate in Washington's Georgetown area. "I went to a builder whose homes I admired (Chastain, a local firm) and told him I'd like to work for him, but that I wanted a base salary.

"He offered me the position of administrative assistant at $18,000 straight salary, or $12,000 plus commissions. I took the $12,000. My commissions should bring me up to $22,000 this year."

Casey handles all advertising for the company, lists the trade-ins (for which she is paid a commission), oversees sales personnel placed in the developments, interviews prospective personnel, looks for land for new developments, does public relations work with local brokers, and attends multiple listing meetings to "give a pitch on our trade-ins and on our developments."

"It's an eighteen-hour-day sometimes," she repeated. "But I love it. I'm single. A woman with responsibilities at home couldn't handle a job like this. But that's the great thing about real estate. You can set your own pace."

Not every woman is anxious to work an eighteen-hour-day or compete ("Scared as *Hell*," one woman described her emotions) with women who list $300,000 houses without batting an eyelash or choking on their chlorophyll mint.

Many women hesitate to be caught alone in a commercial-industrial warehouse with twenty men, or in country mud with even one man.

Not every woman is emotionally prepared to zip her parka, climb into a snowmobile, and show another woman twenty acres of ice, while assuring her through chattering teeth, "You'll never be lonely, dear. There's an Eskimo family living less than fifty miles from your front doorstep."

"Fly clients to Fiji, or 'Titla-whatever!!" one new agent exclaimed when informed of Irmgard Patterson's exploits. "I'd have to divorce my husband and put my children in an orphanage!"

Shirley Klein has taken her Florida real estate license and found "the perfect job for me."

Shirley works four hours a day—Monday through Thursday—and two hours on Saturday morning as "reservations coordinator" for the highly successful Century Village East at Deerfield Beach, Florida. For her eighteen-hour work week she receives a straight monthly salary of $900, plus a flat $50 commission for any sale resulting from her initial contact with a client.

"Our company advertises in out-of-state and Canadian papers," she explained, "giving an 800 toll-free number to call to those interested in coming down as our guest to look over the condominiums and the amenities offered. If I make a reservation for a client, and he is subsequently sold a condominium by one of the sales staff, I receive $50 out of the sales commission."

"Can you give me an average figure on your commission checks?"

She opened a drawer, and looked through her file. "Here's one for over $200, another for over $300, and I've made well over $400 some months. A good average, I suppose, would be between $300 and $400 a month."

Shirley is in charge of her department, and has two women and one man working under her, on salaries of $150 a week, with the same commission arrangements—$50 for every sale resulting from a reservation made.

"Their monthly commission checks average out about the same as mine. We all work the same number of hours."

With her Florida real estate license, Shirley has a stable eighteen-hour work week, and an income of approximately $1,250 a month.

"It's the real estate license that makes it possible," she said. "I have friends working as secretaries five days a week, seven hours a day, for half the amount of money."

"I'm home when my husband is home—and not too tired when I get there. Not too tired to enjoy Florida living.

"Incidentally," she added, "this type of job is excellent for an older widow, who isn't interested in knocking herself out."

There are many low-key ways for the woman uninterested in becoming "Ms. Real Estate, U.S.A." to use a real estate license. Scan the papers, talk to the firms in your area, large and small. Attend seminars and workshops to find the area of real estate best suited to your needs and lifestyle.

"Get your license, and then use it the way that's best for you," Shirley Klein advised.

"And once you get your license, for God's sake, don't let it expire!" said a California woman preparing to take her license examination for the second time. "I got mine twelve years ago, worked for a few years—making the best money I've ever made—then got so busy raising two husbands and three children I let it expire. In California, you can put your license on ice for a small fee. I suppose it's the same in other states."

North, South, East, and West, women advise: Get your real estate license. If circumstances make it impossible to put it to use now, investigate your respective states for the procedure required to place the license on inactive status.

It may very well be the best insurance policy a woman can have.

# CHAPTER 13

## Money Opportunities for Women in Building, Developing, and Restoring

> Homes are the business of women,
> whether keeping them, selling them or
> building them.
> Helen Scott, president,
> Helen Scott Custom Builders

### What's a nice girl like you doing building houses?

Woman's place is not necessarily in the home—nor even in selling homes. Her place may very well be building homes, the late Grace Perego told a group of real estate women in 1927.

Broker Perego, one of the outstanding women pioneers of real estate, started her career building flats in San Francisco before World War I, graduated to apartments, and went on to commercial building. During World War I she traded one of her apartment buildings for a California ranch and launched a successful career in country real estate. She employed women exclusively in her brokerage firm.

Following the example of Grace Perego and Cora Foster (who built homes in Houston before the turn of the century), a few women figuratively climbed on the roof during the thirties with a hammer in their hands and nails between their teeth. An increasing number during the forties learned that flashing is not indecent (as long as it is used to protect against seepage), that rafters support roofs—not floors, that a mud sill is not necessarily something children muddy with their shoes, that not all foundations are sold in "Ladies Lingerie." And, that not all studs are put out to pasture. For some women, closed sheathing became as familiar as open closet, sole plate as familiar as hot plate, and ridge board as familiar as bread board.

By 1949, the National Association of Home Builders marked women's emergence as homebuilders by staging a half-day, all-women builders' program at its annual convention in Chicago. The event drew a capacity crowd of men and women, with an overflow of three hundred turned away.

Lillian Moebus of Brooklyn, chairman [sic] of the Women's Council of the National Association of Realtors legislative committee, called for more personal interest by women builders in their respective cities and towns. Particularly should they see that any beginning of a slum area was corrected, Miss Moebus said. Constructive action, by women, she argued, was the "defense against socialism in housing."

Realtor-builder Maude Butler, of Tulsa, Oklahoma, drew a big round of applause from the women when she pointedly told the men builders present that "women want dining rooms." They also, she told the men, wanted three other things—closet and storage space, an entrance hall, and good circulation in the house plan.

She had three thousand women to back her up. For three thousand women had told her in a survey what they wanted in a new home. She tested their answers by building a seven-room "Home of a Thousand Suggestions." It was visited by one thousand people on opening day, sold on its third day, and was written up in such journals as *American Builder* and *Practical Builder*.

*Parent's* magazine gave Mrs. Butler's home its "Merit Award" for best home for family living during the annual convention of the National Association of Home Builders in Chicago in 1951. Her entry was judged on its excellence of plan in terms of arrangement, use of space, storage facilities, and provision for equipment to produce the greatest livability for an American family with two or more children.

## Breaking into today's market.

You'd like to sell homes with adequate closet and cabinet space? Homes with kitchens that do not require the short-order cook to also be a marathon runner to make it from stove to table to refrigerator?

You're embarrassed about your explanation that the contractor (spelled ex-carpenter) thought putting gold carpeting in the living room, green carpeting in the dining room, and red carpeting in the bedrooms gave the house "a lot of class"?

You're tired of wondering with puzzled clients why the house has no linen closet; why the family room is the size of a postage stamp while the dining room will accommodate a sit-down dinner for twenty-four nicely; and why the washer and dryer space is next to the television space?

Mary Harpley of Akron, Ohio (1977 president of Women's Council), has been an agent since 1958 and a broker since 1961. Her specialty—residential sales. About six years ago she formed a construction company.

Why?

"It was frustrating to sell homes with obvious defects. I had built my own home twice, purchasing the lots, having the plans and specifications drawn up in accordance with my ideas and subcontracting it out. Each time I was pleased with the results, and reaction from friends and clients was favorable."

"Would you encourage other women to go into building?"

"Definitely. Women are aware of what a home should offer the purchaser. Building homes is going to prove to be a natural for women—just as selling homes became a natural for them.

"It's far more stimulating for the woman with a creative bent than selling," she continued. "You see a lot, visualize the type home that would fit well on it. It's exciting to see that first shovel of dirt turned and the framing rise. The most exciting and rewarding stage of all—from a woman's point of view—is choosing carpeting, wallpaper, colors, light fixtures, hardware, etc.

"Building is a challenge—a different world from selling homes someone else has built."

Several roads lead into Mary Harpley's "different world." You may buy a lot, subcontract the house out, and try to sell it—becoming a speculative builder. Or you may elect to sell the house first by getting your customers to sign a building contract—becoming a custom builder.

The amount of capital needed will depend on the type of building business you plan to set up, your state laws, and the cost of the land in your particular area. Fayetteville, Arkansas, builder Pauline McKinney can buy a residential lot for $6,000 to $7,500. In Beverly Hills, lots haven't sold for that since Douglas Fairbanks, Sr., hunted coyotes on his property in 1919.

If you have a good financial statement, it is possible to become a speculative builder by clearing a lot and obtaining a construction loan on your subcontracted plans and specifications. This type building has advantages and disadvantages over custom building. It is usually easier to sell a completed house. The customer can see what he is getting. It is difficult for the average buyer to visualize furniture in a home, looking at a set of blueprints. But, there is always the risk of delay in selling your completed "spec" home—or homes. The speculative builder must have enough capital to keep up loan payments for a reasonable time.

The custom builder puts up a house or building under contract with an owner.

If you're starting as a custom contractor—building a house for someone on his lot—you will be paid a percentage of the total price at the completion and inspection of certain stages. How much, and at what stages, will depend on your contract with the buyer and on the practices of the financial institution making the loan to your buyer.

The modernization and rehabilitation field takes less capital at the start—unless you're using labor, brick masons, carpenters, etc.

Procedures vary by state, but the following architectural and engineering steps apply in most states:

1. Complete plans and specifications of the house you intend to build (to be submitted for building permits and for approval by FHA, VA, or whatever financial

organization may be asked to make the loan).

2. Development of the plot plan and siting the house on the lot.

3. Coordination with survey's transit to see that the house is put in the right place, and that foundation and walls are true and square according to plans.

4. Control and supervision to make sure that construction is completed according to plans and specifications.

For those not wishing the expensive source of an architectural firm for architectural and engineering planning, a number of famous architects have put out portfolios of designs of various types of homes. Plans and specifications for any of these houses can be purchased from the architect at a reasonable cost. You will need a local surveyor or engineer to survey the site and to make any modifications in the house plan required to adapt it to the site or to local building requirements.

Most real estate women in construction serve as general contractor, subcontracting the entire house out, relieving themselves of the responsibility of labor and materials. Lots are purchased, plans drawn up, required building permits obtained from various agencies, blueprints and specifications put out to subcontractors for bids, and the entire package submitted to a lending institution. The city or county inspects after each phase—foundation, framing, etc.

Mary Harpley builds "spec" homes priced from $50,000 to $100,000. She seldom has more than one home under construction at a time. All of Mary's homes have been subcontracted.

"Do the male subcontractors resent having a woman as general contractor?" I asked.

"If they do, I'm unaware of it. They know I go back a long way in homes.

"But you can't be a general contractor from behind a desk or by using a phone," she said emphatically. "I have no problem telling construction men what to do—if I see something wrong, see that they're doing a slipshod job.

"They'll move on to another job, but my name will be connected with that house as long as it stands, and I'll be responsible for any defects for one to two years from completion. There is talk of a five-year warranty.

"I tell my subs that if they see something wrong with the plans or the layout to 'tell me now!'

"If I build a house that doesn't move, my profit will be lost to high interest rates on my construction loan. If a woman can't speak up to the extent of protecting herself, the building business is not her area."

For the woman interested in building on a larger scale, the Small Business Administration may be a source for funds. Previously the SBA denied loans to builders on the grounds that the home-building industry was "speculative." Under recent regulations, SBA is now authorized to guarantee loans to builders to finance new construction and to acquire existing buildings for substantial rehabilitation.

The regulations state that a firm contract of sale will not be required in advance of construction or rehabilitation if the demonstrated purpose is immediate sale. The loans, made on a deferred participation basis, must be repaid within eighteen months, plus estimated time for construction or rehabilitation. Assistance will not be granted for site acquisition or land development costs, except on-site utility connections. A bill seeking approval of SBA loans to builders for rental housing and for site acquisition and land development costs is now before the Senate and House.

### How to lose your blouse in building without really trying.

You like blue carpeting? Put it in throughout the house. Those experts could be wrong about "average taste dictates."

An "open feeling" gives you a sense of "freedom"? Eliminate some of those walls—open it up! Those same experts could be wrong about the average person desiring privacy in the bath.

You've hungered for a quiet house? Why not triple the insulation throughout? Prospective buyers may appreciate the silence—if not the price. You've yearned to exhibit your knowledge of the latest trend in building, and at the same time prove your patriotism? Put in every new energy-saving device known to man or woman, workable and unworkable.

Make sure you put in every labor-saving device you ever dreamed of having in your own home—practical and impractical. Show no partiality in this area. And, make sure all materials used by your subcontractors are of the highest price—if not the highest quality.

No better method has yet been devised for losing your blouse in speculative building than the time-worn one of building each house as if the same person were going to occupy it for the next one hundred years. Namely, you.

Helen Scott of Norton, Ohio, has been in real estate since she was twenty-two. She entered as a secretary-bookkeeper, became an agent in 1964, began building in 1967, and obtained her broker's license in 1971.

"If I couldn't find a house a prospect liked, I'd take the prospect to a builder. In 1966, I was responsible for fifteen homes being built by a local contractor. Invariably, I served as an unpaid consultant with regard to carpeting, colors, paper, tile, etc. It dawned on me one day that I could have built the homes myself rather than being satisfied with the small referral fee the contractor paid me."

The first few homes Helen built in 1967 were speculative and priced around $28,000. She had four or five going at the same time, she said, on a few scattered, moderately priced lots she had bought. She does custom building exclusively now, with her average home contracted for around $80,000.

At one time she had her own carpenters, but now subcontracts her homes. "I would advise women coming in now to subcontract everything out. It saves you a lot of time and trouble—wear and tear. It eliminates labor and material woes. If you try to have your own crew today, you must have an excellent office staff to take care of the paperwork alone. If you subcontract, you write one check."

## America's "make-over mania."

Architecture, psychologist Jung observed, is the "foam" society leaves behind when the wave of life ebbs. America's love affair with the past has reached an emotional apex in the desire to rescue, restore, and rehabilitate the nation's "architectural foam."

Throughout the country spacious homes and well-constructed commercial buildings are being made to fit modern needs for less than the cost of new structures. The rapidly increasing number of Americans eager to work or live in these older properties when properly restored has resulted in a burgeoning field for the broker-builder able to bring together these two forces.

For years, certain areas around the country suffered neglect. Large homes were divided into multiple-family dwellings or allowed to disintegrate into eyesores. A few properties were rehabilitated during the forties and fifties, but it was in the sixties that interest in older properties accelerated.

Financing for reconstruction was difficult to secure at one time; however, lenders have found that clients interested in redeveloping were good loan risks and that property values accelerated, providing increased security for loans. In officially designated historical areas, funds may be available on a matching basis from the federal government.

The money comes from the National Park Service under authorization from the National Historic Preservation Act of 1966. Most of the money is ticketed for the more historical buildings and museum type of restoration, but funds are also available for other restoration projects. State officials with the Department of Land and Natural Resources are encouraging more use of federal funds by private land and building owners.

For certain areas of San Francisco and Sacramento, the architectural foam of the nineteenth century is "gingerbread" Victorian. The price of these homes, originally built for a few hundred dollars from pattern books titled "Cheap Dwellings" has soared in the past few years. In established Victorian areas, such as San Francisco's Pacific Heights, it is estimated that the price of a Victorian has gone up 15 percent a year since the mid-sixties. In developing Victorian areas, such as parts of the Haight-Ashbury district, a home that sold nine years ago for $27,000 is now listed at $120,000.

The first Victorians were built in the mid-1800s—

simple wooden box-like homes similar to a five-year-old's drawing of a house. They were painted dark gray at the base to imitate a granite foundation, and lighter gray at the top to imitate stone. Only the window sashes were painted a dark color. Over the years, elaborate ornamentations were heaped on the original squared-off box design. From street level, a false front extending a few feet above the actual roof gives the impression of a bigger home. From the side, the house hints of a Hollywood western movie set.

Finding a Victorian with promise of rehabilitation sometimes requires several months' time. Termites, dry rot, weak supports, and crumbling foundations are common. Securing financing on a property that may have little more than a remnant of plumbing can be a challenge, and escrows may stretch through decades of title changes. In spite of these drawbacks, agents report that there is a daily increase in the demand for such properties in Northern California.

The experience of Maryland builder Perry Van Vleck testifies to the demand for restored properties, and the opportunities in this area. Mr. Van Vleck rebuilds houses that were old when the ink on the Declaration of Independence was still wet. He has turned 105 acres of meadowland on the outskirts of a tiny seventeenth-century Patuxent River ghost port, Lower Marlboro, into a typical early colonial village. Just thirty-five miles from the White House.

"In Accomack County, Virginia, everywhere I looked I saw beautiful deserted Georgian houses, weeds growing right up to the doors, unwanted and ripe for vandalizing," said builder Van Vleck. He bought five of the homes, and since they were too far from Baltimore and Washington to interest anyone, he made plans to have them moved to Lower Marlboro.

Not all the homes in Lower Marlboro came from Accomack County. Some were brought from western shore Maryland counties, among them a 1704 tavern known to have been visited by George Washington.

Builder Van Vleck finances his homes too. The average buyer puts down about $30,000, and makes monthly payments on the balance. He contends that he's giving people more for their money than they'd get in a new house in the area. He has a waiting list for the less expensive restorations. "I could sell ten tomorrow," he said.

### Recycling commercial structures.

"The hottest area in commercial real estate today is the recycling of existing small shopping centers and strip developments," according to Alan Herd, University of California consultant on real estate education. "Knowing the procedures of making these conversions is an outstanding tool for an investor or real estate broker."

One of the reasons Mr. Herd cited for the boom in recycling is that developers don't have to fight a no-growth municipal policy with conversions. In a converted center, the zoning problem has been virtually overcome—it is there for the existing center.

"Creative opportunities exist for weak, old, or just obsolescent centers to be upgraded. Many stores can be enlarged or reconfigured and leases can be rewritten profitably to conform to new retailing practices and consumer trends. The developer saves enormous improvement costs on existing parking, utility connections, improvements and lighting. Traffic access is also there and generally doesn't have to be reconfigured."

An old bank becomes a theater, a building that once

served as a schoolhouse now serves as corporate offices. A streetcar barn is converted to a shopping center, a city hall to a restaurant. A railway station to another restaurant. An abandoned corner gas station is transformed into a modern office building.

Marjorie Taber of Darien, Connecticut, vice-president of Realtech Corporation, and manager of the Barbara B. Clarke Realtech division, recently sold a 66,000 square-foot mansion, carriage house, and two guest cottages built in 1902 for a near $3 million price tag. The property, located at the end of a peninsula jutting out into Long Island Sound, will be remodeled as a private association with eight owners sharing the costs of maintenance, including landscaping, the sea wall, pier and roads.

Marjorie Taber calls it "the most exciting transaction I have ever participated in, made doubly rewarding by the rehabilitation opportunities it involves."

In Santa Ana, California, the sixty-year-old Santora Building, once the finest office structure in town, has been restored. "It looked dismal," said Henry Stotsenberg. "Neon signs covered the building, windows were painted over, wrought iron was in bad shape, oakwood floors were covered with linoleum, and skylights were covered with twenty years of pigeon manure. It was very dingy and dark."

Mr. Stotsenberg, along with Alan Beall, president of Blackfield Hawaii, is also involved in the restoration of the Yokohama Specie Bank building on Merchant Street in Honolulu. Beall plans to get $60,000 of the restoration money on a matching basis from the federal government.

### Resources for restorers.

The greatest stumbling block on the road to restoration was once the problem of finding old materials and objects needed for the project.

*The Old House Catalogue* (published by Universe Books) now rounds up 2,500 products, services, and suppliers for restoring, decorating, and furnishing the period house, from early American to the 1930s.

If you don't know how to find hand-hewn beams or antique bricks, thumb through your catalogue. You'll find that the beam is available in four- to twenty-five-foot lengths, and can be shipped; that there is a warehouse of old brick, and if you decide to settle for "new old bricks" they can be matched to existing old brick in size, texture, and color.

If rotted clapboards on an old house must be replaced, a supplier can provide the real thing in weathered five-inch strips. If the metal iron work needs replacing, there is new cast iron work in traditional designs for use on porches, balconies, and gates in American, French. Spanish, and Colonial styles.

Paneled wall fireplaces in Eastern pine like those that appeared in many Colonial homes may be obtained.

Moldings, railings, balusters, spindles, newel posts, veneers, inlays and hardware are yours for the ordering, and most any type mantle is available, including authentic Victorian styles and Art Nouveau designs, plus all the accouterments—reproductions of coal scuttles, fire tools, and andirons. There is even information on old authentic paint colors.

Obviously, specialization in historic properties is not for everyone. The woman contemplating a career in this area must have a sincere interest in such properties. Exhaustive research on her part is necessary. She must have a crew of carpenters and painters adept at working with older properties. And her subcontractors must be chosen for their ability to make these older properties fit modern living standards without disturbing the esthetic values.

## Counseling your buyers on architectural foam.

Your buyer's investment—or your investment—in rehabbing or restoring a property can only be justified if the property's earning power and value is substantially increased by the renovation.

Anthony Downs, chairman of the Board of Real Estate Research Corporation, advises that the area around the building is the key to whether rehabbing is a good investment.

"Clearly," he said, "the best moment at which to invest in rehabilitating structures in any neighborhood is just after property values have begun to rise, but before that fact has been widely perceived. Many local property owners do not realize property values in the area are shifting from a downward to upward trend until long after the shift has occurred."

The key to spotting such a trend, Mr. Downs believes, is a combination of accurate information about the neighborhood, good judgment about local housing conditions, and "just plain good luck." But, he recommends the following principles to help make good judgments:

Avoid low-rent neighborhoods considered undesirable because of adverse social conditions such as high crime rates or dominance by very low-income households.

Seek areas in which rents are low because the properties are older, run down and generally undistinguished, rather than because the neighborhood is considered positively undesirable. Watch for the following characteristics:

1. Presence of at least some recent "pioneering" re-habilitation by households.
2. Absence of major problems of personal security.
3. An uptrend in local property values.
Seek areas that have these plus factors:
1. Location near potential anchors such as parks, lakefronts, downtown, or universities.
2. Dominance by owner-occupants, especially if they have organized a community organization to promote neighborhood interests.
3. Commitment by the local government to neighborhood improvement.

Mr. Downs also recommends looking for amenities that appeal to adults. That means shopping, dining and entertainment facilities desired by young unmarried people and young married couples without children or with preschool children.

If you follow his advice, and unless unorthodox or unusual changes are made in improving the property, you can expect its sales value to rise in a direct ratio to the money spent for remodeling.

The value of a home increases most by the upgrading of a kitchen or bathroom, the addition of a bathroom, an extra bedroom or a new family room.

If you are restoring an older building for clients, urge them to capitalize on the age and dramatize some of the old architectural features. Too often, in an attempt to modernize, unique and attractive features are destroyed or covered up.

There's an old saying—"If you have a defect, dramatize it, don't hide it." When modernizing bath-rooms and kitchens try to capture the past century charm.

Highlight the high ceilings, architectural molding, old fireplace, window details, hardware and doors; yet, be as contemporary as you desire in the furnishings, colors, accessories and art. Remind buyers that modern furniture shows off well with a background of an earlier period. One dramatic way to achieve this is to select a dark color for the walls with a light colored wood trim and white high ceilings.

## Your future in building, developing, restoring.

Six figures for a house? It wasn't many years ago that people spending $100,000 were either very wealthy or living beyond their means—set apart by extravagance and luxurious lifestyle. The $100,000 house is no longer rare. It is advertised regularly in local newspapers and magazines and more "spec" builders are venturing into the high end of the residential building market and finding ready buyers—of all ages and life-styles. They have two common characteristics: the desire for a comfortable home and the financial ability to purchase it.

But, many women builder-Realtors believe that the average cost of new homes has become dangerously high.

Land costs are the prime culprit in driving the cost of homes up, Helen Scott said. "The cost of a finished lot in many areas is responsible for 25 percent of the sales price of a new home."

Next on her list of culprits—"bureaucratic regulations" (federal, state, county, and local). "It takes months, sometimes years, to process the scores of applications and forms through federal, state, county, and local bureaucracies in order to get a new development approved."

Environmentalists, Helen believes, are trying to overcome two hundred years of deficiencies in a five-year period, and without regard to economic conditions and housing needs.

"For instance," she said, "in 1950, a twenty-two-foot roadway was required for a subdivision. Now the requirement is sixty feet.

"While wider streets, more parks, more open spaces are desirable, they nevertheless are helping to make the American dream of owning or building a new home out of reach for many American families."

"What can you do about it?"

"Become involved politically at the local level," Helen said. "Homes are the business of women— whether keeping them, selling them, or building them."

Considering the number of women in residential re-sales, building new homes, or restoring old properties is a relatively "untouched field" for women. Yet, it is a natural for the woman broker specializing in residential properties—or for the woman broker into commercial industrial.

"You have three ways to go," said Helen, "three ways to make money. Your client usually has a home to sell. You list it. He needs a lot—you sell him the lot. Then you build his new home on the lot you've sold him. Beautiful!"

# CHAPTER 14

## Exciting Career Opportunities for the Young Woman

*My God! How little do my countrymen know what precious blessings they are in possession of.*
Thomas Jefferson

*The young woman coming in.*
*Will they buy a house from you?*

If you are a young, single woman entering the labor force, government statistics indicate you will work forty-eight years of your life—if you remain single. If you marry, your sentence may be reduced from forty-eight years to twenty-three.

Those same government statistics reveal that about one out of eight households in the United States is now headed by a woman, and the number is on the rise. As women assume more responsibility, they become more motivated to generate enough income to keep their financial responsibilities above water.

Organized real estate is fully cognizant of the fact that like other industries they must recruit and retain more young people between the ages of twenty and thirty-five; that young people are an asset to a firm in terms of profit, inspiration, and innovative ideas.

"More young people would be attracted to real estate if they could come in on a salary," said a recent female university graduate. "Men, as well as women.

"Some of us are aware that earnings in real estate can be fantastic, compared to other fields, but after four years of 'getting by,' we're desperate for a steady paycheck."

She had considered real estate at one time, during her college years. "But," she asked, "how could I compete with those sharp, middle-aged women who're going to town in residential sales. They have an advantage over a young person, male or female. They know what homemakers are looking for. And buyers trust a mature salesperson more readily."

Do they?

Carol Delzer is twenty-six years old. She was twenty when she obtained her agent's license, twenty-two when she became a broker and established her own Northern California firm. She oversees a staff of ten— including her mother. Her other agents range in age from twenty-two to thirty.

"People used to point me out," said Carol. " 'Look! There's that twenty-two-year-old broker!' But, no more. There are many successful young people in the business now."

Why does she hire young agents, rather than more mature ones?

"Because young agents are easier to train. They're more open to suggestion—not 'set in their ways.' But, my mom," she added hastily, "is my top producer."

Most of her firm's business is with young couples and young single men, Carol said. "I have a better rapport with people my own age, and there's a big market there.

You have the young couples with children wanting to get out of an apartment, and young bachelors aware that it's to their advantage to buy rather than rent."

In the last few years, Carol has sold more single men than couples. "The great thing is that you only have to please one person, not two."

"How about single women?"

"They're beginning to come in, too, thanks to the change in credit laws. But the young single man between the age of twenty-five and thirty-five is easy to qualify and is ready to make a commitment.

"And, who can sell them better than a single girl?" she asked with a disarming smile. "If I tell them that their girlfriends are going to be turned on by the fireplace, or the sunken conversation pit, or the bedroom with a skylight, they figure I know what I'm talking about. I doubt if a mature agent would say that to them. And, if she did, they'd figure, 'She's old enough to be my mom. How would she know?' "

Are her young single males buying because it's to their advantage tax-wise?

"Yes, but the great thing going for sales now is appreciation. I lean heavy on that. I remind them that the rent they're paying covers all costs of property ownership for their landlord, plus a profit."

"After my young singles have been in their house or condo for a year or so, and watched it appreciate, they frequently become investors—buying a second property from me. They also send other singles my way as investors. My business is now 90 percent referrals."

Expanding to a multioffice firm and increasing her number of agents is not Carol's goal. "My main interest is the acquisition of property," she said.

She now owns half a million dollars worth of real

estate in the Sacramento area—all acquired since she obtained her license six years ago. Her holdings are in residential properties—single-family dwellings, duplexes, and fourplexes.

"I run an ad on contract with a local paper every day stating that I buy equities. I get a call at least once a week from someone asking me to come out and look at their place. If I'm interested in the house, I usually offer them $500 for their equity, and the rest on paper. I use maximum leverage because the appreciation on residential property has been fantastic."

"Are there other opportunities open to the young woman broker, aside from investing?"

"Yes. If she knows the business and is a good, entertaining speaker, the biggest money-making thing going now is the 'educational seminar.'

"I have a friend, a man, who commands $5,000 to conduct an all-day seminar—$3,500 for a half day. Although he's very knowledgeable on the subject of real estate, he has not done what some women in this business have done—started from scratch and built a successful business, or pyramided their investments into a sizable estate. But, he's a terrific speaker—almost an entertainer, and that's what the Realtors want who put these things on."

The seminars are usually sponsored by a board, Carol said, with each participant paying a certain fee.

"The speakers are seldom women. Women are taking over the business—in residential sales—but the men are up there telling them how to do it!"

Carol thinks that the women would like to hear it from another woman. They will hear it from Carol in the next few years if her plans work out. She has taken a course in public speaking, and recently delivered her first hour-long dissertation on the subject of building a real estate business to a group of newcomers under the auspices of her local board.

"By the time I'm twenty-eight, my cash flow from my investments should be such that I can devote my time to conducting seminars and handling my investments," she said.

## The burgeoning singles market.

In 1970 singles owned only 17 percent of American homes. By 1976 the singles share had risen to 23 percent. It is estimated that 65 million singles with incomes of $15,000 to $40,000 will enter the market between 1978 and 1980, and that by 1980, 50 percent of both new and used homes will be sold to singles.

What will your single clients look for in a home? Young Gail Stoorza is owner-president of the Gail Stoorza Company Marketing Communications of La Jolla, California. The single-story home and an open floor plan with the kitchen flowing into an entertainment center is favored by single buyers according to Gail. A large master bedroom is preferred, with a second bedroom that can be used as a den or office. Wet bars, private patios, abundant storage space, and built-in shelves are also in demand.

Gail's research uncovered a resistance to the swinging singles' complexes of a decade ago. Today's young professionals, she said, prefer a normal environment similar to where they grew up. They are not interested in being isolated as a distinctive social class, and they do not favor large developments. They seek a natural population mix of single and family, old and young, within a wide range of life-styles.

## Home loans and the single girl buyer.

Ten years ago, a young single woman expressing a desire to buy a house rather than a dress might have found herself on a couch with a psychiatrist nearby—or in front of an x-ray machine with a technician instructing, "Remove your earrings and place your forehead against the plate."

The new federal equal credit laws have created a new market in real estate—the young, single woman of moderate means. Lending institutions have been stampeded by women borrowers, coborrowers and advocates for equal treatment of women in the mortgage market.

Like her feminist namesake, thirty-two-year-old Susan Anthony of Los Angeles is at the forefront of this new women's movement.

"In 1973," said Susan, "there was no way. I went to every bank in town. They said, 'Absolutely not. We do not lend to single women.'"

With the relaxation of credit laws, Susan found a house that fit her financial capabilities as a $900 a month administrator. When she recently sold the home to buy another, her loan application was approved in twenty-four hours. She admits that her good payment record on the first house helped, but maintains that she noticed a definite change in the lender's attitude.

Statistics gathered in a California study done by Investors Mortgage Insurance Company of Boston give some indication of the trend. In 1974, one out of every thirty-five home loan applicants was a single woman. By 1980, IMIC President Jackson Goss said, 10 percent of those applying for home loans will be single women.

"The earning power of today's single woman, as well as her increased interest in home ownership, has made her as acceptable a loan candidate as her male counter-part."

Another factor attracting more single women to home ownership is the increasing popularity of the condominium. IMIC found the single woman loan applicants prefer multidwelling settings, because they offer advantages of security, maintenance-free housing and built-in social opportunities.

Pat Scott, a Realtor for thirteen years in Southern California, has watched the change occur. "Ten years ago, a woman who was not a professional wouldn't have been able to get a loan. Today that's not true," said Pat.

One federal housing loan rule, now rescinded, directed that when a married couple applied for a loan, only part of the woman's income could be counted, making her sort of a half-person in the endeavor. Lenders used this percentage rule, too, Pat said grimly. "I remember the good old days when a woman to count her income had to get a letter from her doctor saying she was not pregnant and was practicing birth control."

Growing numbers of women entering professional ranks have brought about another appealing item—the combining of homes and office, providing a hard-to-beat long-range investment.

Jackson Goss cited IMIC research figures which showed that women lawyers and doctors in California increased by 23 percent over 1975 and passed the six-thousand mark. He also noted that this state's home-seeking unmarried women are mostly in the thirty-five and under age bracket and 68 percent are college educated.

### The exciting world of office leasing.

You don't know how many cupboards a kitchen must

have for your ad to read "marvelous cupboard space"? And, you don't give a damn?

You don't think Mrs. Hardtoplease and her four children will fit into your Honda? And you don't want them to fit?

Consider office leasing.

Young commercial-industrial broker Jan Campbell, of Honolulu, leasing agent for the opulent restored Yokohama Specie Bank building on Merchant Street, calls leasing the "income arm" of her business. The bread and butter.

"It's exciting. Stimulating. You're doing business with business," Jan said.

Her three female associates, Andie Zaehring, Mary Hanlan, and Sidnie Miller, all under thirty, echoed her words.

Jan's firm specializes in restaurant, office, and industrial properties from Mapunapuna to Ala Moana. Finding the right location, price and atmosphere for the young company can be very rewarding—personally and financially, she said.

"They'll continue to use your services throughout their growth period—hopefully until they've reached the maximum of their requirements."

"You seldom meet a woman over thirty-five in office leasing," said Marilyn Wolfe of Atlanta. "It's an area young women can enter on a salary, plus incentive. For the young woman just out of college, it's a more 'career oriented' area than residential sales. And, while not everyone comes in on a salary, some developers prefer this method."

Dark-haired, attractive Marilyn handles clients from the prospective stage through move-in. She leases space, does floor-plan designs, selects interior materials, and works with the general contractor on space completion.

"In residential sales most of your contact is with women, who're spending their own money. But, in office leasing you work with men who're spending someone else's money. It's an entirely different area, one that requires a different training program.

"If you call on Bethlehem Steel you have to know what they have, what they need. We cover everything—types of walls, amenities, insulation, etc.

"If a man asks a question about construction, you must be able to answer it. If they ask what module your building is built on—10 foot or 8 foot, you can't sit there with your mouth open.

"A physician needs extra plumbing, a dentist lead lining in the walls because of the x-ray equipment. Your training program is ongoing. You must spend time on the job-site talking to construction people, the contracting and developing departments of your real estate firm, architects, and engineers."

What college courses can a woman take looking toward a career in commercial leasing?

"Basic business administration, real estate appraisal, business law, among others," said Marilyn Wolfe, who worked as director of training and employment for an industrial relations firm before entering office leasing.

Is leasing a good background for commercial-industrial brokerage?

"Definitely," she said. "It gives you a head start in the commercial-industrial field. And, that's where the money is for young women coming in—in my opinion."

Does office leasing resemble conventional residential sales in any way?

"Yes," according to Marilyn. "One of the most important aspects is the necessity of properly qualifying prospects—as in residential sales. How many square feet does he need? If he needs 40,000 and you don't have it, you're wasting your time and his.

"Another way that office leasing resembles residential sales is the necessity of following through. I call a mover for my clients if it is appropriate, I always go to see them after they've moved in and take a plant. You want to keep them there—or if they need to double their space, you want to put them in their new quarters."

Will the men try to bait you?

Frequently, according to several young women in the business. A woman in a leasing office was once a highly unusual sight—a surprise to the male behind the corporate desk. You probably need to know more than your male counterpart, simply because you're a woman.

Are there any advantages to being a woman in a male-dominated area?

Yes. It's easier to get in, but after you get in, you've got to be better than a man.

If you are single, will your challenging job scare dates off?

Most men will find your conversation far more stimulating than one in which you relate how many pages you photocopied that day.

Will they understand if you have to turn them down because of business?

Most of them—especially those in the business world themselves.

Will you hear, "You're awfully young," from businessmen?

Possibly. You must have an air of self-assurance—no matter your age. Youth can be a disadvantage because you may have to sell yourself before your product.

What other advantages does a woman have?

Your advice on furniture placement, colors, etc., is a

plus. Your male competition does not usually spend time on this aspect.

Will you run into "What's a pretty girl like you doing in a man's world?"

Many times. But, don't become defensive.

Are male prospects likely to stray from the subjects of construction, interior details, and length of lease and onto the color of your eyes and your measurements?

Some. But, handle it tactfully. If you're not interested in him personally, make him aware that you *are* interested in his business.

Should you take your male prospects to lunch?

Try to steer clear of lunch dates in order to avoid embarrassing the man who feels uncomfortable about allowing a woman to pay his lunch check. Most people are at their best in the morning—in their office.

Are secretaries less receptive to a woman than a man?

Yes. But try starting a conversation about something that might interest her—something not related to your reason for being there.

"Is office leasing a good area for women?" I asked a young male corporate executive.

"If a woman is competent, I prefer working with her on this type of thing. Women take a more personal interest in what the office is going to look like. They give the added service of helping with drapes, colors, carpeting, etc.

"If a woman is sharp, and has that added magic quality known as 'empathy' a man will open up to her more than to another man. Women are good listeners. That's where they have it all over the men.

"We spend most of our day with other men. It's a nice change to have a woman enter the office.

"Let's face it," he said with a frank grin, "men just naturally prefer talking to women.

"If she knows what she's talking about!" he ended emphatically.

# CHAPTER 15

# What's Ahead in the Most Fantastic Career in the World for a Woman?

*The single family dwelling. Will it survive?*

As attractive and remunerative as various other areas of the industry may prove to be for some women, the great majority of women are in residential sales. Most women entering will do so through residential sales, and the majority will remain there.

Is your career in residential sales in danger of being buried alongside the beloved single-family dwelling? "No," say the experts.

Real estate is a basic commodity, and your career in residential sales is in no danger of succumbing to the dread disease of inflation, or the creeping paralysis of lack of demand. The American dream of ownership of a small piece of land and a home on that land led to the settlement and prosperity of the country. Americans today are no different from their ancestors in this aspect.

You are selling the best bargain of its kind in the world today—the model and standard for nations worldwide. Your buyers expect and find central heating and air conditioning, advanced kitchen appliances and bathroom fixtures, special storage and utility rooms, garage space and superior insulation; amenities not found in the average home in any other nation.

The price of a home in West European nations is now from 12 to 25 percent higher than in the United States. Mortgages in the United States are obtainable with as little as 5 percent down. In Europe and Japan they run around 40 to 50 percent down on higher priced homes. On the average, in Europe and Japan, the down payment is about $23,000—nearly $20,000 more than required by United States lenders.

How does the home you're selling compare in size?

The average American home now has approximately 1,600 square feet of space, while the average European home is several hundred feet smaller.

Economist Anthony Downs is chairman of the board of the Real Estate Research Corporation, a subsidiary of the First National Bank of Chicago. He is consultant to the Brookings Institution and the Ford Foundation, and numbers among his private clients Standard Oil of Indiana and Inland Steel Corporation. No less an authority pronounces your career in residential sales safe.

According to Anthony Downs's calculations, if 60 percent of the American people were priced out of the market, leaving 40 percent of our households able to afford a new single-family home, that would be *28 million households!*

"This whole argument," he said, "about pricing people out of the market presupposes that households can only spend 25 percent of their incomes on housing, and they have no other assets to spend. But, many households have resources that they've inherited from their parents, or borrowed money from their parents, or they have capital received by making a profit on the sale of an existing home and they use that for a down payment. They just don't rely on their incomes. And, furthermore, many more households have two people earning income, so they can spend more than 25 percent of their income on housing."

By 1980, purchasers of homes may first have to come up with the down payment on $100,000, then get in line in some areas of the country. That's the scenario offered by two homebuilders, Ken Agid, of Newport Beach, California, and Milton Kettler of Washington, D.C. Both have recently had the experience of holding a lottery because they had such demand from buyers that a drawing of lots was the only fair way to distribute the limited supply of houses.

Builder Agid developed one of the hottest selling projects in the country on the Irvine Ranch in Orange County, including one development with a waiting list of ten thousand qualified prospects.

"The demand has resulted in the cost of housing rising 2 percent a month," he said. "We are in the position where it takes us four years to get zoning, four months to build a house and four minutes to sell it."

Ann Mauvais of the small university town of Davis, California, began an innovative marketing technique that has mushroomed, and could be applied in university or college towns across the nation by enterprising real estate professionals.

"Our office," Ann explained, "was deluged with requests by parents to find rental homes for their children while they attended University of California at Davis. It just didn't seem logical to me to have to add all that rent to the other expenses of education.

"With a present 12 percent real estate appreciation factor in the area, it seemed to me to make a lot more sense to have the parents buy a home, or cosign with their student, then sell it when the youngster graduated. The appreciation would have to absorb a major portion of the educational expense. The student owner could rent out rooms to three or four friends to reduce his monthly payments to practically nothing.

"The idea made sense to a great number of parents. They referred other parents and students and this unplanned 'specialty' service of our office grew. By now we have had several instances where the 'temporary' home has passed to the third child in the family."

## New developments. Added insurance for your career.

*The second mortgage. Unexpected plus for the homeowner.*

Bankers who wouldn't discuss second mortgage loans a few months ago, are now leaning eagerly forward in their chairs.

Once used to reduce the cash down payment required when purchasing a home, the second mortgage has suddenly evolved into a popular and viable method of obtaining needed cash—and, at reasonable interest rates.

Debts are being consolidated, cars and boats purchased, new furniture acquired, kitchens remodeled, bedrooms and baths added, vacations taken—all financed by second mortgage loans.

The reason for the dramatic increase in second mortgage loans? The rapidly rising values of homes. As values go up, often at 1 percent a month, equities go up, increasing the owner's capability to borrow funds. A home purchased for $45,000 two years ago is probably worth close to $56,000 today (much more in some areas). That extra $11,000 makes beautiful collateral in the eyes of a lender!

*The graduated mortgage. Is it what your buyers need?*

Under the new "graduated mortgage payment" home financing plan, HUD is authorized to insure three thousand graduated payment mortgage loans over a twelve-month period for single-family home loans and condominium loans insured by FHA.

The plan makes possible lower monthly payments during early years of the loan's life, starting with an amount less than the interest charge alone. The monthly amount increases each year for a five- or ten-year period, depending on the precise plan selected, then levels off for the remainder of the life of the loan.

The primary objective is to give young couples a break. Many families who would otherwise have trouble meeting monthly payments of a conventional fixed-payment plan can live with this new kind of payment schedule.

As an example, a family might purchase a home and execute a thirty-year, $35,000 loan at 8.5 percent interest. If the plan selected called for a 3 percent annual increase in payments over a ten-year period, the monthly payment during the first year would be $223—$46 less than the payment on the same loan, but with a conventional fixed-payment plan.

The monthly payment would increase 3 percent to $230 the second year and 3 percent each succeeding year through the tenth year. On the eleventh year, the monthly payment would level off at $300.

The outstanding principal amount due on a graduated payment plan loan actually increases during the initial years, as the unpaid interest is added to the mortgage balance. Slightly larger down payments may be required in some cases to insure that the balance does not exceed the maximum loan amount.

## Beneficial changes for your veteran buyers and sellers.

Even though your veteran clients may have used their G.I. Bill benefits to buy a home once, they're now entitled to sell that home and buy again with the same low down-payment financing.

This change in the law opens the door for many veterans to invest in real estate. If they have owned a home for a few years, they will likely have enough appreciation in value and equity to put into a good investment property, financing it with a conventional loan. Then, they can buy another house for their own use under the G.I. Bill with little or no down payment.

Conrad Sweet, broker with the Toni Lavan Agency in Dolton, Illinois, specializes in such investments. Here's how he helped veterans in two recent cases.

"We had a veteran with a little slab house he originally bought for $17,000 on a V.A. guarantee. There was no down payment. Today the house has appreciated in value to the extent that we sold it for him for $34,000. He took about $20,000 out of the deal in equity and appreciation. With that $20,000 he was able to buy a six flat that will pay him a nice income and give him tax advantages. And, he also bought a bigger home with no money down because of his V.A. guarantee.

"In another case, a veteran sold his first home and bought a duplex for $40,000. Again, there was no money down, but now he owned his own unit plus another one that pays him $200 a month in rent."

Veterans can use the loan guarantee program to buy up to a four-unit building, as long as they occupy one of the units. The rents from three units will generally cover mortgage payments and taxes for all four, so the owner in effect lives in his unit free.

"If you called one hundred veterans who bought homes with a V.A. guarantee in the last twenty years, not more than five would realize they could sell and buy something better and probably have money left over to invest.

"A veteran client must be able to qualify for the mortgage, just as any other buyer," he pointed out. "A veteran making $8,000 can't buy a $40,000 building because he would not be able to make the payments."

There is sometimes a problem getting a seller to agree to let a veteran use the V.A. program, because the law prohibits veterans paying points (a one-time charge equal to 1 percent of the mortgage). The 3 or 4 percent fee that a lender charges must be absorbed by the seller, not as in conventional loans, by the buyer. But, it's a matter of education.

"A veteran usually pays the full appraised price," he continued. "Other buyers, knowing they are going to pay the points on a conventional loan will offer less than the asking price and negotiate it. The seller might pay three or four points, but he gets a better price for his house. It all works out the same in the end."

According to a V.A. loan guaranty officer, the only requirement for a veteran to buy another home is proof of sale and a paid-off mortgage on his previous house. Then they just apply for a certificate of eligibility, and they are restored their full benefits.

### The home warranty program— new protection for all.

A home warranty program has been initiated by the

National Association of Realtors, making it possible for your buyers to receive protection against defects of a home's major components for a period of at least one year.

While the main objective of the program is to assure buyers protection against certain types of defects which may not be discovered until after purchase, the collateral objective is to protect Realtors, Realtor-associates, and their seller clients from liability based on alleged failure to disclose defects in the property or on misrepresentation of the condition of the property.

The program provides that an inspection of the property be made about the time the listing agreement is signed. In the event of a defect, or failure in one or more of the property's elements which has not been disclosed in the inspection report, the buyer has claim for reimbursement from the insuring company.

If your seller wishes to participate in the program, a professional inspection by an approved inspection company will be made and a report will be issued stating that all components of the property can be covered or that the property can be covered with one or more of its elements excluded.

The seller then has the option of bringing the deficient components up to standard, buying the contract with the exclusions or declining to purchase the coverage.

If your buyer finds a defect in a component covered in the warranty program, he pays the first $100 of the repairs, with the warranty company paying for the balance of repair or replacement.

Cost of the program for the seller, including the inspection and warranty contract, is presently in the $100 to $125 range for one year's protection.

## *What's it like in other countries?*

Ebby Halliday, of Dallas, serves as vice-president of the Residential section of the International Real Estate Federation.

"Are women a force in real estate in other countries?" I asked.

"The number of women in the industry in all other countries combined is insignificant compared to the number of American women in the business," she said.

"And, those who do come in must be extremely competent. The requirements are much greater, there is not the ease of entry found in America. For instance, it takes years of formal education to become a broker in England and Australia.

"At the international meetings you will find perhaps a dozen women representing various countries. France will have a few, Sweden, West Germany, Taiwan, Australia. But, you find scores of American women."

The most visible women in the profession in countries outside the United States are "born into real estate," Ebby said. "There's a very competent woman in Austria. Her father and grandfather were in the business. And, she has a law degree."

The Halliday firm is the largest wholly owned residential real estate company in the world. Foreign nationals are aware of the accomplishments of American women, particularly in the residential area, and are impressed. Ebby was invited by the Australian Institute of Real Estate to speak to a group of women in Sidney and Melbourne in an effort to encourage more to enter the field. "About two thousand Australian women attended," she said. "Most of them university women.

"Worldwide, people in the business are interested in learning how we 'do it' in America. I remind them that the success story of American real estate and the men and women engaged in it, stems from the fact that we are blessed in our country with a free flow of brokerage.

"Professionals are very restricted in most other countries," she added.

This "free flow of brokerage" and the entrepreneurial spirit found in the practice of American real estate is the envy of real estate professionals worldwide. In Holland, where there are a handful of women engaged in real estate (and not many more men compared to the number in this country), real estate commissions are set by the government. Three percent: 1-1/2 percent is paid by the seller, and 1-1/2 percent by the buyer—maybe. If one of the consumer organizations has informed the buyer that he cannot be legally forced to pay his share, the commission is 1-1/2 percent rather than the customary 6 percent found in America.

In Greece, there are only 1,500 real estate professionals in the entire country! This situation was brought about, say the experts, by the imposition of a myriad of government rules and regulations. Example: No real estate professional is allowed to engage others to work for him. Several may be allowed to occupy the same office and split costs, but each must work independently. Commissions are negotiable between all parties, and can run as high as 5 percent—as low as 1 percent.

If a real estate professional gets a buyer's name on a contract in Norway, before the deal can be closed, the government must be given "first refusal."

In France it may take two years to obtain the government's permission to tear down your own building. And, your investor would not be allowed to evict a tenant from his apartment building between October and March—no matter how many months tenant may be behind in his rent, no matter if the neighbors report that he's chopping up the doors and cupboards for firewood. The government's reasoning? It's too cold outside.

In Brazil, your leasing principal must have a guarantor who owns an apartment somewhere—which presumably would be confiscated if the client did not pay his rent. His bank, even if the largest in the world, won't do. The guarantor must provide a copy of the deed to his home, his latest property tax statement, the registration of his home and a statement of precisely how much he makes a year, including salary and other assets. No secrets. An investigation is made, not of the lessee's ability to pay, but into the ownership and property value of his friend's place! In downtown Rio de Janeiro, the process of simply getting a telephone (the real estate professional's most important tool) involves the expenditure at the very least of $1,000.

Can it happen here? Yes.

According to one of the nation's top builders, Milton Kettler, of Washington, D.C., the cost of housing has risen to unprecedented heights in the past few years due to government requirements that extend the time needed to build, regulate what can be built, how it is built, and where it is built.

"A builder no longer deals with the potential buyers of the house—he deals with the bureaucrat who makes the decisions about what he can build.

"On a recent project, we had to deal with twenty-two federal agencies to get approval. They are more inclined to reject a project than to tell you to go ahead because they take less risk if they turn it down."

Referring to his townhouse project in an expensive section of Washington, he said, "Our move back to the city was related to the problems of dealing with officials in the suburbs. We were at the mercy of one county, and we decided that it made sense to diversify geographically to avoid the problems that might arise for us in that single area."

What can you do to help maintain American real estate's free flow of brokerage and entrepreneurial spirit?

Membership in the five-hundred-seventy-five-thousand-member National Association of Realtors makes you a part of the largest trade organization in the world.

"Individually we're small business, with all the problems that beset that segment of the business community," said Patty Mattoon of Pittsburgh, successful broker, and a leader in organized real estate. "But collectively we're one of the largest industries in the nation, and we can have tremendous impact."

A tax system favorable to real estate investment, an open economy, ease of transferring ownership, leverage, and moderate property-use restriction, are some of the advantages investors have found so attractive in American real estate. Protection—not only against inflation, but against expropriation, political instability and collapse—is the prime motivating factor in American property's popularity among foreign nationals. Thousands of investors have watched their holdings disappear in Algeria, Angola, the Belgian Congo, Cuba, and nations too numerous to name. In Rhodesia, investors are becoming increasingly nervous, and capital is flowing out of Italy as the Communists draw near to power. A few cautious Swiss, it is reported, are looking at farm land in our Middle West, in case of the political collapse of Europe.

By becoming active in organized real estate locally, on the state level, and nationally, you can make sure that the advantages that have made American property the most coveted item in the world marketplace are not lost.

*Will you sell your house in Muleshoe
and move to Beverly Hills?*

Will you cover your office typewriter and uncover the stimulating field of office leasing?

Cease measuring dresses and commence measuring houses?

Sweep the last candy wrapper, gum ball, and child out of your car and head frantically for the nearest warehouse?

Walk out the door onto the land because you agree with Marie Sullivan that "no one has been there to spoil the beauty"?

Move from moderate-income housing to a broad spectrum of commercial and luxury properties as has Flaxie Pinkett, and echo her words: "The most important thing I've proven is my competence."

Sell your grocery store and become an investment counselor to overseas Chinese?

Establish your own real estate school?

Polish your public speaking, and work out a schedule with your travel agent for nationwide educational seminars?

Establish your own firm? Enlarge to a multioffice firm? Remain small?

Concentrate your energies, and your license on the acquisition of income-producing properties?

Follow Gene Rasmussen of Houston and Mary Floyd of San Diego into the more relaxed, but no less remunerative area of on-site or subdivision selling?

Become an authority in the area of government housing, as has Daisy Donovan of Detroit?

Pick up your blueprints and venture into building and restoring?

Hire a research economist, a public relations man,

have a psychiatrist standing by, and face the bureaucrats for a career in developing?

You are engaged in what has been described as "free enterprise in its purest form." There is no limit to your growth potential as an individual, or professionally. Women are now responsible for an estimated 70 percent of all residential sales, and the Harvard-MIT Joint Center for Urban Studies predicts that new U.S. households will increase by some *22 million before 1985.* Experts agree that the United States is on the verge of a housing boom that will increase at a faster rate than the gross national product over the next five years.

Whether the Equal Rights Amendment is passed unanimously by fifty states or defeated ignominiously by half a hundred states is not germane. Your battle for equality has been won by the competence and drive of thousands of women. Many dollars have flowed into male pockets from the efforts of women since the "house woman" went out for coffee, kept the front windows free of fly specks and the mens' desks free of dust. Women capable of turning over millions of dollars worth of property each year are in no danger of being told to go home and mend their husband's socks.

Rose Marie Garrison, a lifetime member of the industrial division of Atlanta's Million Dollar Club, doing business in the male world of warehouses, factories, and offices believes that women owe as much to the men who have helped them, as they owe to their own perseverance. "Men deserve a lot of recognition and credit," said Rose Marie. "If it were not for their open-mindedness and willingness to recognize and encourage potential, we wouldn't be anywhere in this business."

Patty Mattoon served as the first woman president of the Greater Pittsburgh Board of Realtors in its sixty-four-year history. "Women have succeeded in real estate," she said, "because of our ability to work not only with buyers and sellers but with other members of our industry. We do not differentiate between men and women."

How successful a woman becomes now depends entirely on her own ability and initiative. The last barrier is down. The front door is open—as is every other door in the industry. You are free to soar as far, as high, as your empathizing, ego-driven (spelled competent) wings will carry you in real estate—the best way, the quickest way, the safest way, the only way, according to Marshall Field, to become wealthy.

Margaret Crispen has been an active investor in commercial and residential properties and unimproved land since the mid-fifties. She holds a real estate license in the state of California. She spent two years researching the career opportunities for women in real estate, and this book is the result of that research.

The widow of an American Air Force officer and the mother of two daughters, she has lived in London, Bangkok, Taipei, and five states in her own country.

# BOOKS FOR THE SUCCESSFUL WOMAN

**THE WOMAN'S SELLING GAME: How to Sell Yourself—
and Anything Else**
By Carole Hyatt                                    (#97-195-2; $4.95)

At some point every day, a woman needs to sell something to someone
—from a prospective employer on herself or her ideas to her boss, to
her husband on a vacation or a child on going to bed. Hyatt, leader of
the famous "Woman's Selling Game" Workshops, shows you how to
sharpen your natural selling skills so you can sell yourself—and anything else—better.

**HOW ANY WOMAN CAN GET RICH FAST IN REAL ESTATE**
By Margaret Crispen                               (#97-254-1; $4.95)

A practical guidebook that will show you exactly how to make it in real
estate. How to get started, how to get into commercial/industrial real
estate, how to invest in real estate, going into business for yourself,
how to use your license to get an important salaried job, making money
in developing and restoring—and much, much more.

**THE BEST WAY IN THE WORLD FOR A WOMAN TO MAKE MONEY**
By David King and Karen Levine                    (#97-515-X; $4.95)

David King, founder of "Careers for Women," shows you how to have
a career in executive sales. He explains how to select the industry and
sales climate that are best for you; how to be the most desirable candidate for the job you choose; how to make a sales presentation; how to
organize yourself and manage your time—and many more practical
guidelines.

**THE WOMAN'S DRESS FOR SUCCESS BOOK**
By John T. Molloy                                 (#97-572-9; $4.95)

Leading wardrobe engineer and dress consultant John T. Molloy shows
you how to dress to get the extra edge you need in business. He tells
you what to wear for what occasions, how to dress in different cities
and for different kinds of jobs, what colors are best for business effec-
tiveness, what kind of makeup and hairstyle work best, and answers
all the questions you may have on dressing for success.

# MORE WARNER BOOKS OF INTEREST

**GAMES MOTHER NEVER TAUGHT YOU: Corporate Gamesmanship for Women**
By Betty Lehan Harragan                    (#81-563-2; $2.50)
"At last—the definitive, hard-nosed manual on corporate politics for the career woman! This is the one book every woman *must* read if she's serious about moving ahead in her career."
—Womanpower Newsletter

**BOSS LADY**
By Jo Foxworth                    (#91-252-2; $2.50)
The author, president of her own advertising agency in New York, gives realistic and workable advice on how to make it to the top in business. "Tells how to get there, how to stay there and what to expect on the way. Full of wit, humor and frankness."                    —The Oregonian

**SEXUAL SHAKEDOWN: The Sexual Harassment of Women on the Job**
By Lin Farley                    (#91-251-4; $2.50)
A ground-breaking book that tackles the serious problem of sex discrimination on the job and what you can do about it. "A significant contribution to our understanding of the forces working against the working woman."                    —Washington Post

**THE CHANGING LIFE OF THE CORPORATE WIFE**
By Maryanne Vandervelde                    (#91-180-1; $2.50)
The handbook for the wives of upwardly mobile men. Psychotherapist Vandervelde provides a manual for women who play important roles in their husbands' careers yet seek independence for themselves. "No subject is taboo—mental illness, alcoholism, even sex . . . the corporate wife needs all the help she can get. Like this book."
—Baltimore Sun

**BLACK MACHO AND THE MYTH OF THE SUPERWOMAN**
By Michele Wallace                    (#91-262-X; $2.50)
A powerful analysis of the black macho mystique and the vulnerability of black women that results from it. "She crosses the sex/race barrier to make every reader understand the political and intimate truths of growing up black and female in America."                    —Gloria Steinem

# MORE WARNER BOOKS OF INTEREST

**GETTING ORGANIZED**  (#97-182-0; $4.95)
*By Stephanie Winston*
A clear, easy system for organizing almost every aspect of your personal and professional life. How to deal with paper, space, time, money, and much much more. "All you need is this book . . . it delivers precisely what it promises."
—*Mademoiselle*


**RECIPES FOR BUSY PEOPLE**  (#91-542-2; $2.50)
*Kelly Services, edited by Sylvia Schur*
A special cookbook for people who don't have time to waste when they cook. Culled from over 10,000 entries, the 300-plus recipes in this book range from ultra-simple lunches to gourmet feasts—and all of them quick as can be.


**TELEPHONE TECHNIQUES THAT SELL**  (#97-453-6; $4.95)
*By Charles Bury*
Shows you how to use your most powerful business tool, your phone, to maximum advantage. Using case histories, check lists, and action plans, Bury gives you all the information you need to handle telephone inquiries, get appointments, generate business—and add more power to your everyday conversations.


**WORKING SMART: How to Accomplish More in Half the Time**  (#95-273-7; $2.75; June)
*By Michael LeBoeuf*
A practical, entertaining handbook that offers hundreds of well-organized, concrete action-ready ideas and techniques for insuring a high return for every bit of your working time and energy. Shows how to set specific goals on a daily and long-term basis and allocate your time accordingly.


**HOW TO SELL ANYTHING TO ANYBODY**  (#82-957-9; $2.25)
*By Joe Girard*
"The World's Greatest Salesman" (*Guinness Book of World Records*) shares his secrets of success. He tells you how to close a deal, how to keep a customer for life, how to make direct mail and word-of-mouth work for you, and much more.


If you wish to order any of these books, please send a check or money order for the price of the book plus 50¢ per order and 20¢ per title (N.Y. State and California residents, please add sales tax) to Warner Books, P.O. Box 690, New York, N.Y. 10019. Please allow four weeks for delivery.